RAY HYMAN

Professor of Psychology, University of Oregon; author of books and articles in the areas of methodology, information theory, perception, creative thinking, and unorthodoxies; researcher in the areas of cognition, judgment, creativity, and esthetics.

The Nature
of Psychological Inquiry

PRENTICE-HALL, INC., *Englewood Cliffs, New Jersey*

THE NATURE OF PSYCHOLOGICAL INQUIRY, *Ray Hyman*

PRENTICE-HALL FOUNDATIONS
OF MODERN PSYCHOLOGY SERIES
Richard S. Lazarus, *Editor*

PRENTICE-HALL INTERNATIONAL, INC., London
PRENTICE-HALL OF AUSTRALIA, PTY., LTD., Sydney
PRENTICE-HALL OF CANADA, LTD., Toronto
PRENTICE-HALL OF INDIA PRIVATE LIMITED, New Delhi
PRENTICE-HALL OF JAPAN, INC., Tokyo
PRENTICE-HALL DE MEXICO, S. A., Mexico City

Designed by Harry Rinehart

C-61069(*p*), C-61071(*c*)

Foundations of Modern Psychology Series

The tremendous growth and vitality of psychology and its increasing fusion with the social and biological sciences demand a new approach to teaching at the introductory level. The basic course, geared as it usually is to a single text that tries to skim everything—that sacrifices depth for superficial breadth —is no longer adequate. Psychology has become too diverse for any one man, or a few men, to write about with complete authority. The alternative, a book that ignores many essential areas in order to present more comprehensively and effectively a particular aspect or view of psychology, is also insufficient. For this solution, many key areas are simply not communicated to the student at all.

The Foundations of Modern Psychology is a new and different approach to the introductory course. The instructor is offered a series of short volumes, each a self-contained book on the special issues, methods, and content of a basic topic by a noted authority who is actively contributing to that particular field. And taken together, the volumes cover the full scope of psychological thought, research, and application.

The result is a series that offers the advantage of tremendous flexibility and scope. The teacher can choose the subjects he wants to emphasize and present them in the order he desires. And without necessarily sacrificing breadth, he can provide the student with a much fuller treatment of individual areas at the introductory level than is normally possible. If he does not have time to include all the volumes in his course, he can recommend the omitted ones as outside reading, thus covering the full range of psychological topics.

Psychologists are becoming increasingly aware of the importance of reaching the introductory student with high-quality, well-written, and stimulating material, material that highlights the continuing and exciting search for new knowledge. The Foundations of Modern Psychology Series is our attempt to place in the hands of instructors the best textbook tools for this purpose.

Acknowledgments

In writing this book, I have benefited from the suggestions of Barry Anderson, Fred Fosmire, James Jenkins, Richard Lazarus, Richard Littman, and James McGaugh.

Contents

Contents

Contents

xi

The Nature
of Psychological Inquiry

Method and Content
in Inquiry

"The idea is a seed; the method is the earth furnishing the conditions in which it may develop, flourish and give the best fruit according to its nature. But as only what has been sown in the ground will ever grow in it, so nothing will be developed by the experimental method except the ideas submitted to it. The method itself gives birth to nothing." (Claude Bernard, 1865.)

Psychological inquiry consists of a number of different kinds of activity. One is the formulation and selection of problems for investigation; it is this activity that gives an investigator his creative role. A second type is the

3

1

making of observations and the collecting of facts that are relevant to a problem; this endeavor lends support to the popular stereotype of the scientist as a technician who mixes chemicals in test tubes, bombards elements in cyclotrons, and reads pointers on dials. A third is the processing and analysis of the facts; this fosters the picture of the scientist as a fellow who juggles numbers, fits equations, and draws graphs. A fourth is that of explaining or "making sense" out of the data; this gives the investigator the role of theoretician and thinker. A fifth involves communicating or reporting conclusions to colleagues; it is this activity, more than any other, that gives the scientist his reputation for being obscure and difficult to understand.

These steps characterize inquiry in other sciences as well as psychology. What distinguishes psychological inquiry from physical inquiry or biological inquiry are not the kinds of activity as such, but the subject matter—what the inquiry is about. The particular subject matter is what you study in psychology courses—courses that go under such names as learning, sensation, perception, motivation and emotion, socialization, thinking and problem-solving, personality, and intelligence.

That we can and do talk about method and content separately does not mean that these aspects of psychology can be dealt with separately in research. In fact, as we shall note later on, when a psychologist studies a subject matter without careful consideration of how his methods interact with his concepts, he frequently ends up with meaningless or ambiguous outcomes. Conversely, some psychologists become so attached to particular methods that they allow them to dictate the matter of their investigations. Either extreme, of course, results in wasteful research.

Before we elaborate further on the intimate connection between method and content, we should spell out the sense in which we employ the term "content." Any particular inquiry deals directly with unique and concrete events. A psychologist, for example, may turn on a 1000-cycle tone for five seconds before he applies a shock to the foot of a dog. Or he may have a judge sort out a series of colors according to his preferences. Each of these situations is unique and quite complex. The dog may be a mongrel, picked up from the streets, with an unknown history. He may whine, bare his teeth, wag his tail, attempt to scratch a flea, or engage in a number of other movements while the tone is sounding. The experimenter who turns on the tone may be thinking about a quarrel he had with his wife. The judge who is sorting the colors might be recently divorced, suffering from a slight attack of asthma, and participating in the experiment to get his mind off his troubles. All these details, and the many, many more that are connected with the particular events that the psychologist observes, do *not* form the content of psychological inquiries.

Scientific inquiry is not about particular events. Instead, in any inquiry an investigator selects from particular events only certain aspects which are treated as instances of more general, repeatable events. The pairing of a tone with a shock is taken as an example of what is called "avoidance conditioning." After a number of pairings of the tone with the shock, the dog will learn to lift his leg at the sound of the tone and thereby avoid the shock. This relationship between the tone and the leg response is considered an example of a "conditioned reflex"—and it is assumed that this "conditioned reflex" can be established with other animals in other situations. In other words, the psychological inquiry is about something that can be repeatedly observed— a concept and a relationship among concepts. The particular event—this particular mongrel dog in the laboratory on that particular day—can never be witnessed again. But, on the assumption that he is dealing with a "law of nature," the psychologist hopes that the event—pairing a conditioned stimulus with an unconditioned stimulus with the resulting new connection between stimulus and response—is repeatable.

THE INTERACTION OF SUBJECT AND METHOD

Psychological inquiry, like all scientific inquiry, then, is about concepts and their interrelationships. Entire "schools" within psychology can be identified in terms of the kinds of concepts they include and exclude from the scope of psychology. When Wilhelm Wundt founded the first laboratory of experimental psychology in 1879, he defined psychology as the study of the elements of conscious experience. The primary elements of consciousness, for him, were "pure" sensations. To study these primary contents of consciousness, he put adult human beings through extensive training in attending to and reporting only pure sensations—patches of light, odors, sounds— sensations stripped of their interpretation. Later researchers called this brand of psychology "structuralism" and its chief methodological tool was termed "introspection." In addition to Wundt's laboratory at Leipzig, the chief centers of structural psychology were at the University of Würzburg in Germany and at Cornell University in the United States.

Some 30 years after Wundt began psychology as a separate form of inquiry, dissatisfaction with his form of psychology led to new "schools." John B. Watson, in the United States, proposed behaviorism as an alternative to structural psychology. From then on, in his militant program, psychology was to be a natural science. It would not deal with subjective, private experience. Instead, it would focus only on what could be observed as organisms went about solving problems, mastering mazes, reacting to stimulation. What could be observed was behavior—which was made up of such things as glandular and muscular responses to external stimulation.

As psychological history, the preceding two paragraphs are oversimplified and highly inadequate. But they will serve our purpose of indicating the close relationship between subject matter and method. Structural psychology was more than just an emphasis on a particular kind of concept or content— it also implied a particular method for collecting and evaluating data. And this method, introspection, limited psychological inquiry to adult human beings who were willing to go through the lengthy training necessary to learn how to observe their own sensory life. When structuralism was abandoned, the grounds, to a large extent, were methodological. The major technique, introspection, could not produce results that could be obtained in other laboratories. In America Edward B. Titchener could not observe the new conscious elements that the psychologists at Würzburg in Germany had discovered. A bitter controversy erupted. Eventually psychologists abandoned both structuralism as a subject matter and introspectionism as a method.

Watson, too, founded his behaviorism on a method—objective observation of behavior. His "school" ruled out subjective methods such as introspectionism on the grounds that they were unreliable. Psychology as a science had to be based on what could be observed and agreed on by different viewers. Even while he was ruling out certain kinds of data and methods, however, Watson extended the scope of psychological inquiry to include children, illiterates, and animals. In fact, the method of behaviorism could be applied to any creature that could move or "behave" in an observable way in response to external stimulation.

CONCEPTUAL SYSTEMS AS GUIDES TO INQUIRY

These brief comments on structural and behavioral psychologies reveal how the content of an inquiry—its concepts and the systematic context of these concepts—can provide limitations and constraints on acceptable methodology. No inquiry, as we shall see, arises in a vacuum. The psychologist who conducts research begins with some sort of a conceptual system—however vague and ill formed—and ends up with a clearer and better formed conceptual system. It may be helpful to use the analogy of a "mental map" to describe this system. The map, always incomplete and inaccurate, nevertheless provides a rough guide on what to explore and where to point. It helps to provide a *conceptual focus* for the inquiry.

The reverse relationship can also hold. Quite frequently a new method, usually developed in another field, will open up new subject matters for inquiry. Developments in brain surgery, electronics, and miniaturization of electrodes, for example, have recently opened up areas of research into brain mechanisms that were inaccessible to psychological inquiry only a few years ago. Similar impetus for psychological inquiry has come from developments in pharmacology, zoology, mathematics, and statistics. Within the field of psychology itself, important breakthroughs and changes in subject matter have followed the development of techniques for scaling responses, measuring attitudes, measuring meaning, and so on.

Although this reciprocal relationship between content and method exists, it is not perfect. Methods can survive long after the conceptual system that gave rise to them has been rejected or discredited. Such is the case with G. T. Fechner's psychophysical methods for measuring sensory thresholds—these methods are still employed today but within a conceptual framework different from that of their origin. Likewise, conceptual systems can survive inadequate methods—psychologists are still trying to study the mechanisms of thinking but have abandoned the original approach to this task by way of classical introspection.

That methods can be separated from their original subject matter represents a mixed blessing. On the one hand, it is clear that the application of methods developed for one purpose to new subject matters often results in new and creative breakthroughs. This happened in psychology, for example, when Louis L. Thurstone, bored with studying judgments of weight, substituted more interesting stimuli in their place as a way of teaching the psychophysical methods. The result was a whole new field of attitude measurement and scaling that has played a significant role in the development of social psychology as an empirical science.

Unfortunately, the separation of method from content often seems to result in trivial or misleading research. Psychologists frequently seize on a new method without adequately understanding its limitations and the assumptions on which it is based. In employing methods they do not fully understand, investigators often wind up in the ludicrous position of using a technique which assumes a type of relationship that the investigators' theoretical models deny. Some investigators, for example, apply the method of factor analysis, which assumes that individual traits combine additively, to a psychoanalytical theory which clearly implies that traits combine in a nonadditive manner.

In sum, then, the point we want to make is that all psychological inquiry is guided by a conceptual system. This conceptual system—including subject matter, preconceptions, concepts, values, restrictions—serves as a basis for organizing experiments, selecting facts, analyzing data, and interpreting results. Because the conceptual framework limits what the experimenter sees and deals with, it serves both to facilitate and to hinder the development of psychological knowledge. On the one hand, it serves as the necessary background against which to give new facts significance as well as being the basis for determining the relevance of issues. On the other hand, it can also result in failure to see important facts, in missed discoveries, and in the inability to adjust to new facts. The importance of the conceptual system goes beyond its relationship to a particular methodology. The conceptual focus is also what gives unity and coherence to the different activities that form the complex process of psychological inquiry. Whenever an investigator loses sight of his problem, he is apt to get caught up in details of one or another parts of the separate activities and eventually become method-oriented rather than problem-centered. So, as we deal one by one with separate phases of inquiry, you should always keep in mind that the activities themselves become meaningless if they are not continually kept subordinate to, and in the service of, the conceptual focus of the inquiry.

The Process of Inquiry

"But good methods can teach us to develop and to use to better purpose the faculties with which nature has endowed us, while poor methods may prevent us from turning them to good account. Thus the genius of inventiveness, so precious in the sciences, may be diminished or even smothered by a poor method, while a good method may increase and develop it. In short, a good method promotes scientific development and forewarns men of science against those numberless sources of error which they meet in the search for truth; this is the only purpose of the experimental method." (Claude Bernard, 1865.)

8

2

Scientific inquiry is a *process*—a sequence of acts organized around a common focus. In the case of psychological inquiry, this focus is on outcomes that extend our knowledge and command of human and animal behavior. In this book we shall characterize the process of inquiry in two different ways. One characterization will classify the different activities, or *phases*, of the process. The other will classify each of the phases in terms of its *stage* of development—from early to mature. The *phases* are the different activities an investigator performs to gain, clarify, and extend knowledge of behavior. They are the different parts into which we can conceptually separate the process. The *stages* are the levels of development of the investigator's conceptual system with respect to the problem. Not only can we refer to the stage of development of the inquiry as a whole, but we can also refer to the separate stages of development of each of the phases within the inquiry. It can and does happen that some phases within an inquiry are at a primitive level while others are highly developed and sophisticated. We see instances of psychologists investigating a highly formalized and sophisticated theory with rather casual and poorly controlled methods of observation. And we see other psychologists using highly refined methods of observation and data analysis to attack intuitively and vaguely formulated problems.

The stages constitute the historical, or *temporal,* aspect of any inquiry. In the early stages, the process is relatively casual and informal. The different activities within the process overlap and interweave with one another in such a way as to be scarcely distinguishable. Nevertheless, the same kinds of phases are found early as are found later in the inquiry. At later stages, however, the different phases are clearly more differentiated, more highly formalized, and more likely to follow upon one another in a systematic manner. Whether early or late, at all stages of an inquiry we can detect phases corresponding to the following activities: formulating a problem, gathering information, processing information, interpreting information, and communicating information.

The stages of the process can be either the historical development of an inquiry involving several investigators, or the development of a problem in the hands of a single investigator. In this book we shall not distinguish these two kinds of development because similar features occur whether development involves one or several individuals. Likewise, it is possible for a team of investigators to divide the labor of inquiry in such a way that any one individual may contribute to only a few of the phases. Again, for our purposes, it does not seem important to distinguish between individual or team effort. The complete process of inquiry requires all the phases at each stage of the inquiry.

In the early stages of inquiry, the investigator begins with common-sense ideas and concepts from the everyday vernacular. His conceptual framework, in part, is a patchwork of vague beliefs, attitudes, and expectations which he shares with other members of the society in which he was raised. His formulation of these beliefs and expectations will tend to be in everyday language. In addition to the part contributed by his sociocultural heritage, the psychological investigator will come to the problem with ideas and notions that have also been conditioned by his own personal history and experience. He can verbalize some of his ideas and beliefs; others he cannot. His approach to the problem, in addition, will be influenced by a background of unconscious and implicit assumptions and preconceptions. Finally, both his approach and his mental map of the territory before him will be colored by the history of inquiry and speculation on the topic.

This is the conceptual framework within which the investigator makes new observations and interpretations. As he assembles and orders new facts within an existing conceptual system, inevitable changes occur. Finer differentiations are made; new classifications have to be created to account for unexpected or unanticipated items; the conceptual system gradually becomes altered to accommodate the new information. Hopefully, the newer conceptual map that results is a more adequate representation of the "real world."

We can view the process of inquiry as a gradual transition from an initial loose conceptual system to a more adequate and communicable conceptual system of a given area of psychology. The newer system, since it is forged out of observations made during inquiry, presumably is more consistent with the "facts" that have accumulated. In addition, the newer system also summarizes and helps to account for earlier and older facts. Quite frequently it gives the earlier facts a new meaning. And finally, the newer system serves as a convenient guide to new observations and experiments.

THE PLACE-VERSUS-RESPONSE CONTROVERSY

An example of the gradual growth and adjustment of a cognitive map in the history of psychology might be helpful. The behavior of rats in mazes has accounted for an enormous amount of literature in the psychology of learning. Such behavior has also provided endless controversy among different schools of psychologists. One controversy centers around what the rat actually has learned when he finally can run through a maze without error to get his reward of food. For example, Watson, the founder of behaviorism, argued that what the rat learned was a sequence of muscular responses. The psychologist Edward C. Tolman argued that what the rat learned was the "place" where the food was.

The argument goes back to the turn of the century when W. S. Small, a psychologist at Clark University, carefully observed how his rats learned to find food in a maze; he concluded that probably touch and muscular sensations provided the important cues. At the same time, Small noted that when a rat finally learned to run the maze without making any errors, the sequence was not a stereotyped motor pattern. Rather, he concluded, "the central fact in the process seems to be the recognition by the rats of particular parts of the maze."

Both of Small's conclusions—one about the nature of the sensory cues, the other about place learning—provided the conceptual focus for numerous other studies of maze learning as well as stimulating controversies that have lasted to the present time.

Watson in 1907 repeated Small's experiments, but with many refinements and additional controls. Using surgical techniques, he excluded one sense at a time and then observed (a) whether untrained rats could learn the maze and (b) whether previously trained rats could still run it. When he deprived one group of rats of their sight, he found that it impaired their maze learning hardly at all. The same was true of other rats whom he deprived of smell or hearing. Even anesthetizing the soles of the rats' feet and cutting their whiskers did not prevent them from learning or retaining the maze habit. Watson concluded that the essential cues in maze learning must be furnished by the muscle sense, the only one he was unable to eliminate. In addition, he decided that a rat must learn a sequence of responses—each turn serving as the cue for the next turn. Seemingly Watson had disproved the conclusion of Small.

In 1929 Karl Lashley found a way to eliminate the muscular cues surgically. Even though his operated rats, lacking kinesthetic feedback from their lower limbs, had to negotiate the maze with an awkward and inefficient gait, they showed no impairment either in their retention of previously learned maze performance or in learning a new maze. This result argued against Watson's conclusion that the muscle sense was the key factor in maze learning.

The fallacy in the early logic and conceptual focus of these early studies was in the assumption that only one sense could be primary. By the 1930's some psychologists were proposing that a rat will use any sensory cues that are readily available. The rat will employ visual cues, touch cues, smell cues, or muscle cues, depending on the situation and their relevance.

Despite these early conclusions, the place-versus-response controversy flared up again following World War II. A new series of experiments was designed to answer the question: Which is dominant, spatial or muscular cues in learning to run a maze? In general, the results seemed to indicate that rats tend to employ spatial cues when these are clearly available and when a maze is especially complex. But contradictory results still arose. In some experiments, the rats seemed to prefer kinesthetic cues.

A change in conceptualization was suggested in 1957 when Frank Restle applied to the place-versus-response-learning controversy a theory, which he had previously developed for discrimination learning. Restle's theory added a new feature to the issue, for his is a mathematical theory that makes quantitative predictions.* It also suggested that the original issue had been stated incorrectly. Restle's theory and its successful application to the results of previous studies seem to indicate that rats are neither "place" nor "response" learners. A rat, in learning a maze, will employ all discriminable and relevant cues. What determines his rate of learning is the ratio of the cues that are relevant to cues that are irrelevant in leading to the goal. Place and response cues, Restle concluded, add up.

An examination of the history of inquiry on the place-versus-response controversy shows a number of features that characterize the development and refinement of the conceptual systems of psychologists. First, the early conceptualization was oversimplified. The issue was originally stated in either-or terms. Either muscular or visual cues, but not both, must account for learning of the maze. It did not occur to the earlier workers to consider the possibility that a rat might employ all the cues that are available to him. Second, the earlier conceptualization was vague about the boundaries and meaning of its terms. Later work and controversy led to refinements and better classifications of the possible types of cues—for example, an important division was made between intramaze and extramaze cues; thus, when a rat can employ spatial cues in the room, such as a window, it will. Third, some important information was provided only by the perfection of new techniques —such as Lashley's surgical removal of kinesthetic cues. Fourth, even when early critics suggested a more adequate interpretation, as was done by a few psychologists in 1930, they were not heeded. It is only within recent times that psychologists feel comfortable with theories that employ multiple, rather than singular, "causation." Fifth, when the maze-learning problem was shown to be equivalent to another problem that had been successfully solved by mathematical analysis, the statement of the original problem was shown to be almost meaningless and insoluble. And finally, the new mental map not only provides accurate quantitative predictions, and a plausible explanation, but it reinterprets all the previously "contradictory" findings within a new framework; this new map reveals that place and response explanations are not contradictions, but, instead, consistent examples of the same underlying principle.

Later, we shall look at other cases that exhibit similar trends.

THE INTERACTION OF STAGES AND PHASES

The different activities that constitute the total process of inquiry show parallel development with the growth of more differentiated and coherent conceptual systems. Each stage in the process exhibits all the phases, but the earlier stages do not show as clear a differentiation of these phases as do the later stages. At every stage of the inquiry, for example, we can identify some

* F. Restle. Discrimination of cues in mazes: a resolution of the "place-vs-response" question. *Psychol. Rev.*, 1957, 64,217–228.

kind of activity that corresponds to initiating and formulating the inquiry. In the earlier stages this is apt to be something we can best describe as a "hunch," a "speculation," an "idea," or a vague expectation or curiosity regarding a particular issue or fact. Indeed, at very early stages in the history of an inquiry, an investigator might not be able to formulate his question explicitly or state what he is after. In later stages, the investigator may work from models or analogies. These may help him derive "working hypotheses" or predictions concerning observations. At least, they guide him in making observations of a certain kind. In still later stages, the investigator may derive a formal hypothesis for explicit testing. Restle's latest model of the maze-learning situation, for example, leads to some very explicit, quantitative predictions about the number of errors a rat should make in learning a maze when he is given both kinesthetic and place cues instead of just one or the other.

Similar statements can be made about the other phases—gathering data, analyzing the data, interpreting it, and communicating the results. Small's experiment in 1899 did not employ any quantitative measures. The results were qualitative descriptions of a rat's behavior—such as sniffing—as he explored the maze. Later investigations counted the number of errors made on each trial, or the number of trials until mastery. Such quantitative indexes allowed for more explicit comparisons of theories. Restle's model makes explicit predictions about certain features of the data in terms of average numbers of errors and deviations from the average.

The phases in the early stages are not as marked as they are at later stages. Many of them are not even overt—being more a matter of intuition, passive registration of experience, searching of memory, and other prescientific modes of activity. In later stages we see more and different kinds of activity and greater explicitness. The investigator can often formulate his problem, at least verbally. He is now an active observer—the observations being made for the express purpose of providing information relevant to the problem. The data are worked over more thoroughly before empirical generalizations ensue. In still later stages, the phases become even more explicit and demarcated. The formulation of the problem is often a formal matter and involves explicit hypotheses deduced from a broader conceptual system. The controlled observations often involve instrumentation, standardized controls and methods, and explicit rules for procedure. The data analyses are more complex, employing computers and advanced mathematics as well as statistics. Qualitative classification of outcomes are replaced by measurement procedures of increasing power. Explanation becomes formal, abstract, and highly specialized. Even the manner of communication is affected. In the early stages, the communication is still close to the popular vernacular and its models. The general public, or at least the educated layman, can read the original books and monographs without a feeling of being lost or left behind. As a field becomes more specialized, as the knowledge accumulates and becomes more explicitly controlled and formalized, then the audience for the communication changes. The investigator now writes for an increasingly specialized group that consists of other investigators working on the same problem. The communication becomes a journal article rather than a book; the journal article employs special terms and jargon, a uniform format, and so on. The gap between layman and scientist now appears formidable. The scientist has succeeded in achieving an explanation and a system that is relatively free of the tacit assumptions and preconceptions of his prescientific history and wishes. But he has achieved this objective picture at the expense of communication with the remainder of society.

THE COORDINATION OF PHASES

Although we discuss each phase of the process of inquiry separately, we should always keep in mind that effective research depends on the *coordination* of these activities towards a common goal. The various phases, as has already been emphasized, are given coherence by the investigator's conceptual focus. As the investigator becomes immersed in the details of each activity, he sometimes loses sight of the over-all objective. One unfortunate consequence of such immersion in the details of inquiry may be an overemphasis on one or the other of the separate phases. All of us who attempt to teach the art of research know only too well the plight of the student who gets bogged down in the preliminary phase. He never seems to be ready to stop searching the literature, or to finish the first steps of formulating the problem and the hypotheses. On the other hand, we are also familiar with the trivia that result from a hasty plunge into a prematurely designed experiment. Other investigators lose themselves in the intricacies of data-collecting—perfecting apparatus, devising automatic recording devices, becoming enraptured with a polygraph, or reorienting a problem to allow for inclusion of an appealing new gadget. Still other psychologists force the important parts of their labors into highly ritualized, computerized routines for processing data. In their awe of the magic of complex data-handling systems, they lose sight of the main issue. Many of us bog down at the writing phase of the research. Or, even when we succeed in writing up a report that passes by an editorial board, we frequently fail to reach the audiences who would most profit from our results.

Research is most successful only when some kind of balance is struck among the different component activities. With a reasonable deadline before him, an investigator has to allocate resources, time, and effort among these various phases in such a way as to achieve a really significant increment in knowledge about the issue under study. That most of our research, even what gets published, fails to contribute to the development of our conceptual systems merely indicates the difficulty of integrating these various phases into a coherent undertaking. Make no mistake about it. The execution of successful inquiry—in order to produce meaningful and lasting results—is a difficult undertaking. Very few succeed consistently. Even the best of our investigators feel lucky if only a fraction of their ventures pay off.

Getting Ideas

"An anticipative idea or an hypothesis is, then, the necessary starting point for all experimental reasoning. Without it, we could not make any investigation at all nor learn anything; we could only pile up sterile observations. If we experimented without a preconceived idea, we should move at random, but, on the other hand, as we have said elsewhere, if we observed with preconceived ideas, we should make bad observations and should risk taking our mental conceptions for reality." (Claude Bernard, 1865.)

In some ways, instruction on how to do research resembles the description of card tricks in many books on

3

magic. Such descriptions are notorious for their tendency to give only half the story. The standard beginning tends to go like this: "First, secretly get the spectator's chosen card to the top of the deck by your favorite method." Assuming that you are in the fortunate position of having the chosen card on top when the audience thinks it has been lost in the shuffle, the instructions then describe a variety of entertaining ways you can employ to disclose the card to the spectators.

If you are a beginner at card tricks, you probably do not have a "favorite method" of getting the chosen card to the top of the deck; in fact, as far as you are concerned, knowing how to get the chosen card to the top and simultaneously convincing your spectators that the card has been lost in the shuffle is at least half the battle. If you cannot accomplish this first task, and accomplish it well, the remainder of the trick becomes pointless.

Without pushing the analogy too far, we can fairly claim that books and courses in psychological and other scientific research are of a piece with the magic books. In effect, they begin by telling us to first get a problem "by your favorite method." Assuming we have a suitable or important problem, the instruction then tells us how to proceed from there, how to gather data, analyze it, and draw conclusions relevant to the adequacy of our idea. The rub lies, of course, in getting the problem or guiding idea in the first place.

Research can only lead to trivia if the original idea is not worthwhile. Yet, even with the best of ideas, the scientist cannot make a worthwhile contribution unless he is thoroughly grounded in those principles and methods necessary for subjecting the idea to the test of empirical evidence. The success of the card trick requires that the magician first get the right card and then manipulate it in a skillful manner. Likewise, the success of an inquiry depends on the psychologist's first getting the "right idea" and then operating on it according to well-established procedures that collectively go under the label of "scientific method."

THE SOURCES OF IDEAS

The analogy with the card trick must end here. It is easier to specify what we mean by the "right card" than what we mean by the "right idea." Moreover, with a little care and patience, the author of a magic book can describe a number of potentially effective ways for getting the chosen card to the top of the deck. Unfortunately, no one knows how to teach a scientist about getting the "right idea."

In part, our ignorance reflects the current primitive state of the psychology of thinking and creativity. We still know very little, at least from a scientific viewpoint, about how individuals get their ideas. Moreover, as yet, we do not even know how to formulate the problem correctly, or even if it is a potentially meaningful problem. Does it make sense, for example, to attempt to distinguish "successful" from "unsuccessful" thinking? Do "success" and "failure" in this context reflect value judgments rather than psychologically useful principles?

In part, our ignorance is also a matter of the vagueness and ambiguity of the term "right idea." Is it ever possible to state in advance that any proposed idea will turn out to be "successful" in the sense that it leads to research, breakthroughs, or clarification of our understanding of a given domain? To what extent is the "success" of an idea a matter of what the investigator does with it *after* he has formulated it? To what extent does the success of the idea depend on such nonpsychological determinants as the total scientific situation at the time of its formulation, the technological possibilities for its exploitation and development, or the accidents of who happens to be intrigued by it, who is willing to support it?

Whatever the answers to such questions may be, it is clear that current instruction in "scientific method" and "psychological inquiry" emphasizes idea-testing rather than idea-getting. The reason for this bias is apparent. We can specify a number of standardized procedures for evaluating and testing ideas once they have been formulated. We can teach methods for collecting pertinent data under controlled conditions. We can introduce students to a variety of instruments to aid and extend their observing and data-gathering. We can teach routines for summarizing and describing data and for drawing conclusions from the results.

But when it comes to suggesting where or how to get ideas—how to select a problem that is significant or potentially important—we must frankly concede that almost any rules or suggestions we might offer may be completely wrong. Ideas—good ideas—seem to arise from almost any source and at any time. We can point to cases, the more colorful ones, where the idea has struck with dramatic suddenness during a dream or during a period when the investigator was not consciously thinking of the problem. In other cases, the good idea seems to follow routinely from the normal course of carrying out an investigation and then puzzling over its outcome. Ideas occur as accidents, as deductions from theories, as mistakes in reasoning, as consequences of arguments or discussions, as analogies, and even as consequences of some temporary, but abnormal, mental condition.

One thing seems certain. Ideas do not arise in a vacuum. The idea that occurs to a psychologist occurs to him within a given cultural context. Both the psychologist and his idea are products of a political, ideological, technological, and intellectual heritage. In addition, the psychologist or scientist is also immersed within a specialized subculture—the scientific community with its current views, assumptions, and lore. Also, the psychologist, as an inquisitive seeker, comes to any situation with his own idiosyncrasies, a unique history, a particular set of values and motives, and a particular configuration of implicit and explicit beliefs about the way the world is put together. In some manner or other, the particular ideas and hypotheses that an investigator puts forth at any point in time are conditioned by the circumstances of his cultural, scientific, and personal heritage as well as the particular "facts" that now confront him.

To make these various influences concrete, we might profitably trace some of the origins behind one of the germinal experiments in psychological inquiry. The case we shall describe is that of the Russian physiologist Ivan Pavlov, specifically, the events leading up to his famous research on the conditioned reflex. Almost any other case could serve our purpose. However, the background of Pavlov's experiment seems sufficiently well known and striking to make most of the essential points concerning the phase of research that deals with "getting ideas."

THE CONDITIONED REFLEX

Pavlov's classic experiment, performed around 1900, ran as follows. Pavlov and his colleagues would first prepare their subject, a dog, by performing a minor operation which exposed the duct of one of the salivary glands to the external surface of the dog's cheek. After recovering from the operation, the dog was put through several sessions to become familiar enough with the experimental situation to learn to stand patiently in apparatus which, in part, consisted of a loose harness to keep him from moving about.

When the dog was ready for the experiment, which was usually a week or so after the operation, he was placed in the apparatus and the experimenter took up his position in another room where he could observe the dog through a periscope. By means of a mechanical contrivance, the experimenter would start a metronome and then, a few seconds later, would automatically deliver some food to the dog. After a few trials, say five, the animal would salivate a few drops at the onset of the metronome and *before* the delivery of food. With each succeeding trial, the amount of salivation to the sound of the metronome would increase; after a dozen or so trials, the dog would salivate copiously and consistently to the previously neutral sound of the metronome.

In Pavlov's terminology, the consistent pairing of the metronome and the food resulted in the metronome's becoming a *signal* for the food. The sound of the metronome led the dog to salivate in anticipation of the food. The "innate," or "primary," stimulus for the salivation—that is, the food— Pavlov called the "unconditioned stimulus," because it needed no prior conditioning for the elicitation of saliva. Food in the mouth always produced salivation in a hungry dog. He called the newly acquired stimulus, the sound of the metronome, the "conditioned stimulus," because its ability to bring forth saliva depended on the previous experimental conditions which paired the sound with the food.

From this experiment, whose implications drew world-wide attention and debate, Pavlov continued on, for over 30 more years, to devise a variety of elaborations and applications. He demonstrated, for example, the phenomenon of *extinction,* the apparent loss of the conditioned response after several more presentations of the metronome which were *not* followed by food. In a very famous series of experiments, he and his coworkers discovered the phenomenon of "experimental neurosis"—a condition that results when a dog is required to make exceedingly difficult discriminations between conditioned stimuli.

The Origins of Pavlov's Experiment

The question that concerns us is the origin of Pavlov's idea of the experiment on the conditioned reflex. As we shall see, the experiment can be viewed as the resultant of several different influences coming together in the person of this former Russian theological student. For one thing, the conceptualization of the experiment fits directly into the intellectual and scientific climate of the middle 1800's in both Russian physiology and European science. Second, the experiment has roots that can be clearly traced to Pavlov's experiences with particular books and teachers during his school days. Third, his direct impetus was the annoying variations he encountered in the action of digestive glands while he was pursuing an inquiry on a different problem. Fourth, as is invariably the case, an examination of prior history in the field of physiology discloses that the basic idea of the conditioned reflex had occurred to many other investigators prior to its successful exploitation in the hands of Pavlov. Fifth, as is also quite common, the conditioned reflex was discovered independently and almost simultaneously in the United States by a psychologist who was studying the knee jerk. Finally, many of Pavlov's subsequent findings, such as that of experimental neurosis, came about as unanticipated or unexpected side-effects of an inquiry undertaken for another purpose.

Pavlov's experiment grew out of an intellectual climate that had been stimulated by Darwin's work as well as by great advances in the science of physiology. In the middle of the nineteenth century, when Pavlov was growing up and getting his education, Russian physiologists were making great strides. Basov perfected the use in animals of a stomach fistula, or artificial opening, that enabled him to study the digestive processes as they took place. Such an operation was obviously an important guidepost to Pavlov's later work on digestion, which employed the stomach fistula, as well as his work on conditioning, which employed the salivary fistula. Other physiologists of this period were contributing important research to the idea that the digestive system is regulated by the nervous system. Still other work, some of it performed by men who later were teachers of Pavlov, emphasized the role of the nervous system in regulating other organs of the body such as the heart. The idea of "nervism," which this work gave rise to, later became one of the cornerstones of all Pavlov's research.

Another important source of ferment in Western Europe, where many of the Russian physiologists went for their training, was the emphasis of German scientists on the concepts of "materialism" and "positivism." Materialism was the philosophy that all the behavior of animals and men could be reduced to physiological laws (and, ultimately, that all physiological laws could be reduced to physical and chemical laws). Positivism was the faith that science could be applied to the understanding of human and animal behavior in all its manifestations. Pavlov studied under one of these German physiologists, Carl Ludwig, who belonged to a private club whose members swore to rid science of all subjective, supernatural, or nonmechanical explanatory principles.

Pavlov absorbed ideas from this cultural heritage. Throughout his researches on the conditioned reflex, he stubbornly maintained that "psychic" phenomena and "higher nervous activity" must be studied by the objective approach and that all of man's complex behavior and intellectual accomplishments could be explained in terms of the physiological connections between stimuli and responses by way of the cerebral cortex. (This same background influenced the trend of American psychology, which culminated in the formal proposal of behaviorism as the method of inquiry for psychology. Watson quickly recognized Pavlov's conditioned reflex as the foundation on which to build his new objective psychology.)

We can also trace to Pavlov's early education the ideas that eventually resulted in his work with digestive glands and his use of the concept of the reflex as the unit of all higher nervous activity. Many of his teachers, as we have indicated, already were contributing to the idea that the nervous system regulates digestion. Pavlov mentions that at age 15 he was influenced to go into physiology by George Henry Lewes's *Physiology of Common Life*. Among other features of the book, a reproduction of a drawing of the digestive system by Claude Bernard absorbed Pavlov. He began from that moment on to wonder how such a complicated system could work. His interest in the digestive system eventually led to the work on digestion for which he received the Nobel Prize in 1904. And the work on digestion, as we shall see, was the direct impetus to his experiments on the conditioned reflex.

Two additional implications of Pavlov's fascination with Lewes's book are worth noting. The author was a British follower of the famous French advocate of positivism, Auguste Comte. Lewes was especially eager to apply positivism to the notion that psychology can be reduced to physiology. This idea— that psychological phenomena can find their explanation in physiology— remained an important motif of almost all of Pavlov's mature writings. And Claude Bernard, whose drawing was the direct stimulus to Pavlov's interest in digestion, was one of the first men to explicitly suggest the possibility of conducting a study of the effects of psychological factors on salivation. In 1855, Bernard gave several lectures on his research on salivation and described how psychic stimulation could substitute for direct stimulation of the mouth in producing a flow of saliva in a horse. He suggested an experiment with a fasting horse to demonstrate this point. He indicated that one could expose the salivary gland of the horse, in much the same manner that Pavlov later employed on the dog, for making these observations. And Pavlov acknowledged in 1904 that he was aware of Bernard's ideas on this matter.

Among other books that influenced the young Pavlov was Darwin's *Origin of the Species* and Ivan M. Sechenov's *Reflexes of the Brain*. From Darwin, whom he idolized, Pavlov almost certainly borrowed the notion of adaptation of the organism. His approach to the reflex was that the unconditioned reflexes were the result of evolutionary adaptation in the Darwinian sense, but that the potential for the conditioned reflex was necessary to adapt the animal to the fact that food and other important features of the environment can be connected to a variety of arbitrary signs.

Pavlov acknowledged that he was profoundly influenced by an early reading of the Russian physiologist Sechenov's book, *Reflexes of the Brain* (1863). Sechenov, who studied under Helmholz, Bernard, and many other key figures of the European scientific vanguard, maintained that "all acts of conscious or unconscious life are reflexes." In addition, he also argued that the cerebral cortex inhibited the spinal reflexes. Pavlov indicated that, at the time he began his experiments on conditioning, he was not consciously thinking about Sechenov's work. But he believed that Sechenov, at an unconscious level, profoundly influenced his ideas. At any rate, it is clear that Pavlov employed the idea of inhibition by the cerebral cortex and the idea of reducing higher nervous activity to reflexes as the cornerstones of his theoretical outlook.

Psychic Secretions

With all this background,
Pavlov did not plunge into work on reflexes until after a long and successful research career on two other problems clearly based in physiology. His first research concerned the effect of the nervous system in regulating the heart. Then, beginning around 1879, with the perfection of his operation for producing a permanent stomach fistula in a dog, he began his experiments on digestion. In 1897, he published his lectures on this work.

During the course of his work on the effect of the nervous system upon the flow of digestive juices, Pavlov became concerned with the disruption of the regularity of his results by the dogs' anticipation of food before the food was actually placed in their mouths or stomachs. He found this fact distressing because, as a physiologist, he felt that he should focus on the control of the digestive glands by direct stimulation of food in the mouth or stomach lining. Direct stimulation was lawful and clearly within the realm of physiology. The indirect stimulation of digestive flow by the sight of the food or even at the sight of the attendant who normally brought the food, Pavlov, at first, called "psychic secretion." He considered it a nuisance that had to be eliminated.

Pavlov was unhappy with a problem, however, until he had tracked down and controlled every factor that was relevant. He felt that these "psychic secretions" should be studied if he were to learn the entire story about digestive action. Yet he felt uneasy about wandering into this new realm of "psychic secretion." The physiologist Charles Sherrington warned him against doing so, as did many of his friends. After much soul-searching, Pavlov finally made up his mind to take the plunge, and at the age of 53, he began this new line of research that, at first, met resistance and brought him ridicule in his home country. Part of the resistance was from individuals who felt that it was immoral to apply science to higher mental processes. Part was from physiologists who felt that "psychic reactions" were not fit material for a scientific physiology.

At first Pavlov attempted in "psychological" terms to interpret the dog's secretions to conditioned stimuli. He and his colleagues even tried to imagine what the situation was like in terms of the subjective life of the dog. But Pavlov quickly realized that such an approach did not lead to objective and reliable results. He banned further attempts to interpret the dog's behavior subjectively.

As has already been indicated, many earlier investigators observed and commented upon the fact of psychic secretions. In fact, the phrase "watering in the mouth at the sight of food" was well known. Also, in the United States, at about the same time that Pavlov was undertaking his investigations of the conditioned reflex, the psychologist Edwin M. Twitmeyer, as part of his doctoral thesis, uncovered a similar phenomenon. While studying the knee jerk he accidently noted that sometimes, when he struck a bell to warn of the impending tap, a subject's knee would jerk before the stimulus hammer struck it. He realized the importance of this acquired response, and followed it up with further observations and experiments. But when he reported his work to the American Psychological Association in 1904, none of the assembled psychologists under William James's chairmanship showed any interest. Perhaps this lack of encouragement accounts for Twitmeyer's failure to follow up this research.

The Lessons in Pavlov's Story

Before we continue with our discussion of the problem of getting ideas, it may be helpful at this point to pull together some important themes that are displayed in the story of the conditioned reflex. The most important point is that Pavlov's revolutionary experiment was in many ways a product of the cultural and scientific environment in which he was raised. Pavlov's genius lay in pulling together several different threads running through this enviroment, giving them a coherent form and interpretation, and, by a series of patient and brilliant studies, clearly demonstrating their implications. It is important to note that even with the diverse influences pushing Pavlov to the idea that higher nervous activity could be reduced to physiological terms and reflexes, Pavlov took the decisive step along this road only after prolonged investigations of other aspects of nervous regulation of internal organs. It was literally when the issue of "psychic" influence on digestion was forced on him by disturbances in otherwise lawful results that he first, with some hesitation, took steps toward the examination of this issue. Even then, he could not entirely free himself of the still-current notion that "psychic" and "physiological" determinants of glandular flow belonged to different domains. It was only after he was un-successful in attempts to be "psychological" about conditioned reflexes that he was able to bring to bear his prior exposure to positivistic and materialistic thinking. When he finally decreed that the objective approach was the only scientific approach to his problem, however, he did so with the conviction and with the passion that come from one who has been thoroughly indoc-trinated in a positivistic and materialistic viewpoint.

The story also indicates the necessity for patience and devoted application to the goal of thoroughly developing all the implications of a new idea. It is at this step that we can separate Twitmeyer from Pavlov. Both of these men came across different instances of the same phenomenon. Both recognized, in some fashion, the potential significance of what they saw. Both met with discouragement from their first audiences. But Twitmeyer quit. Pavlov ignored criticism, convinced himself that he was dealing with something important, immersed himself in it fully, and devoted the remainder of his life—almost 35 years—to the exploitation of his idea.

BLIND ALLEYS VERSUS OPPORTUNITIES

Up to now we have been treating the activity of "getting ideas" as some-thing that takes place at the beginning of an inquiry. Undoubtedly, the ideas that one has at the very outset of an investigation have most importance for the significance and ultimate impact of the inquiry. But the phase of getting ideas can and does occur at every stage of the inquiry. In the early history of a scientific issue, the origin of ideas is often attributed to such categories as hunch, intuition, the spirit of the times (*Zeitgeist*), the unconscious, a vague sense of discontent, and the like. With further development, the origin of the inquiry can more easily be explicitly assigned to needing to clarify ambiguities or vagueness in existing explanations, filling in gaps in the current store of information, improving the measurement of or isolation of important factors, testing the adequacy of a proposed theory, resolving apparent con-tradictions between data and theory, and so on.

As an inquiry progresses—either from one investigator to another or within a particular study by one investigator—many possible leads and alternatives open up. At each choice point, many ideas occur and many paths or side-issues of potential interest vie for attention. Sometimes, by seizing on an unexpected opening and dropping his main objective, an investigator has made important and significant breakthroughs. But anyone who is familiar with the conduct of research realizes that such potential side-issues occur in great numbers at each step. If an investigator allows himself to be sidetracked by every unexpected observation, he would never bring any inquiry to a satis-factory conclusion. He would be chasing each new lead as it cropped up and running a zigzag course from idea to idea with no continuity and no follow-through on any of these ideas. The dilemma the investigator faces is that of knowing how to select and stick to a significant problem by ruthlessly refusing to be distracted by each new unexpected occurrence. And yet, at the same time, he wants to keep alert and be ready to pounce upon those unexpected "distractions" that really are important. Again we come to an instructional impasse, for there are no rules or guides that can be formulated to tell a budding investigator when to ignore such temptations and when to exploit them.

THE CULTURAL BACKGROUND OF AN IDEA

The process of inquiry can be seen as a continuing activity of trying to assimilate new observations to existing concepts and expectations. As new observations are made during the course of research, they do not, of themselves, lead to new ideas or hypotheses. Rather they serve as catalysts or as reinforcers that arouse or strengthen dormant and existing associations. Pavlov's observations that a dog secretes digestive juices at the sound of the experimenter's footstep could only have meaning in terms of his long and varied exposures to ideas about salivation, nervous control of glands, physiological models of higher nervous activity, and the like.

In this sense, it seems pointless to search for the cause or origin of a new idea. Each of the sources that we have mentioned—the prevailing intellectual climate, the scientific situation, the personal history of the investigator—can most usefully be seen as contributory factors. Each of these sources prepares the investigator to see new facts within a certain light. When a variety of these inputs tends to point in the same direction, when new observations challenge the investigator, the immediate empirical situation can serve as a nucleus around which previously unconnected, but loosely related ideas from these various sources can crystallize. Pavlov's famous experiments and his conceptualization of conditioning represent a fruitful mating of ideas from the physiology of digestion, the physiology of the nervous system, positivism, materialism, Darwin's theory of natural selection, Sechenov's ideas on reflexes and inhibition, and Bernard's ideas about psychic control of salivation, as well as his own previous findings on nervous regulation of nutrition and circulation. The immediate catalyst for this synthesis of varied ideas that were "in the air" was Pavlov's concern about explaining the variations in digestive activity that could not be handled in terms of direct stimulation of the oral cavity.

Many writers have commented on the fact that quite frequently an idea is proposed before the total scientific culture, or the *Zeitgeist*, is ready for it. Thus, Bernard and others clearly stated the idea of the conditioned reflex some 50 years before Pavlov made it into the cornerstone of his research program. Presumably, nothing was done about the idea because the sum of influences at the time did not reinforce it. At least that would be the explanation of those who say the total scientific situation has to be ripe.

When Watson sounded the rallying cry for behaviorism in 1913, the elements of his movement were already existing aspects of the culture. Earlier American psychologists had already recognized the principle that psychology was the study of behavior rather than of experience; that introspection was unreliable; that animal and child behavior were as legitimate subject matters for psychology as was adult behavior. Watson merely brought these elements together and gave them a unitary label and focus at the appropriate moment in the history of psychology.

To the extent that there is truth to this idea of the ripeness of the *Zeitgeist*, we can view the matter in this fashion. An individual's contribution to the field of psychology, through getting and testing new ideas, may or may not be recognized as a significant and revolutionary contribution. At certain times in the history of a field the new idea will fall on deaf ears; at other times it will be seized on as a fresh point of departure. In neither case does it mean that the contribution was either crucial or irrelevant. Some ideas and efforts, although apparently ignored at one time, may help weaken the foundation of an existing system and prepare it for its eventual collapse. Others are more like the proverbial straw that breaks the camel's back. They come as the culmination of a series of prior formulations. Ironically, if an individual happens to be the "first" to propose a new idea (if this were really possible) in a certain field, it is almost certain that he will go unheard. The investigator who gets credit or is recognized as the discoverer, is usually the last one to propose the idea before it finally catches on. In other words, originality, in its ordinary meaning, is not in itself what leads to revolutions and advances in science. Rather it is the ability to pick existing threads and themes, put them together in an attractive and convincing package, and come forth with them at just the proper moment when old conceptual systems have outlived their usefulness and the scientific community is casting about for something better.

From Mysticism to Psychophysics

The case of Pavlov is a particularly good illustration of this last point. Another instructive example comes from an examination of the contributions to experimental psychology made by Gustav Theodor Fechner in the middle of the nineteenth century. Although the official establishment of psychology as an independent and experimental discipline dates from Wundt's founding of the first formal psychological laboratory in Leipzig in 1879, many psychologists date the actual beginning of experimental psychology from the publication of Fechner's monumental *Elements of Psychophysics* in 1860. It was this book, more than any other contribution, that showed psychologists how they could collect and quantify empirical data on sensation. As Boring has put it in his *A History of Experimental Psychology:* *

* E. G. Boring, *A history of experimental psychology.* 2nd ed. New York: Appleton-Century-Crofts, 1950, pp. 294–295.

It is true that, without Fechner or a substitute which the times would almost inevitably have raised up, there might still have been an experimental psychology. There would still have been Wundt—and Helmholtz. There would, however, have been little of the breath of science in the experimental body, for we hardly recognize a subject as scientific if measurement is not one of its tools. Fechner, because of what he did and the time at which he did it, set experimental quantitative psychology off upon the course which it has followed. One may call him the "founder" of experimental psychology, or one may assign that title to Wundt. It does not matter. Fechner had a fertile idea which grew and brought forth fruit abundantly.

What is Fechner's claim to originality? Where did his ideas come from? The first explicit formulation came to Fechner on the morning of October 22, 1850, when he was lying in bed. As a confirmed spiritualist, he saw himself as the enemy of the current materialism of science. In a mystical way, he felt compelled to call upon the world to save itself from the evils of what he called the "night view." On that famous occasion, the idea occurred to Fechner that if he could demonstrate an equation between the physical world and the world of sensations, then people would listen to his argument for the abolishment of dualism and the acceptance of the idea that everything was a manifestation of one spiritual essence. But this insight and its motivation was merely the immediate goal for the synthesis of many ideas then current in the *Zeitgeist*. Boring concisely depicted Fechner's accomplishment as a crystallization of ideas already present in the intellectual climate: *

The times were ready for scientists to get hold of mind by measuring it. Sensory thresholds had been determined as much as a hundred years before Fechner. The physiologists were already experimenting with sensation—Johannes Müller with specific nerve energies in 1826, Ernest Heinrich Weber with tactual sensibility in 1834. To contemporaneous thought Herbert had contributed the notion of the measurement of ideas, while denying the possibility of experimenting on them; and he had made Leibnitz's concept of the threshold well known. Lotze published his *Medical Psychology: The Physiology of the Mind* the year after Fechner's *Zend-Avesta*. It was in this setting that Fechner had on October 22, 1850, his important insight about measuring sensation and relating the measures of sensation to the measures of their stimuli.

Fechner's claim to originality of epoch-making magnitude lies in this insight. His claim to honor lies in his careful and laborious work through the decade of the 1850's, and the crucial character of the *Elements* when it finally came out in 1860. He is credited with having given experimental psychology the three fundamental psychophysical methods still in constant use today, but actually the method of limits goes back to 1700 and may be said to have been formalized by Delezenne in 1827, whereas the method of constant stimuli was first used by Vierordt in 1852. Only the method of average error belongs to Fechner, and that only half, for he and his brother-in-law, A. W. Volkmann, developed it in the 1850's. What Fechner did in the *Elements* was to present the case for sensory measurement and write the systematic handbook for psychophysics, a new field of scientific endeavor.

* E. G. Boring. Fechner: inadvertent founder of psychophysics. *Psychometrika,* 1961, 26, pp. 3–8.

Much is said about a re-straining role of the *Zeitgeist* on scientific discovery. The prevailing intellectual climate can, so it is claimed, stifle new ideas, prevent people from accepting certain possibilities, and resist change. Whether this is good, bad, or both is a much-debated point. We can easily point to cases, such as that of Twitmeyer, where the reaction of a man's contemporaries seemingly prevented or held back a discovery. Yet T. S. Kuhn, among others, seems to suggest that this conservative aspect of the *Zeitgeist* may actually be a necessary condition of scientific growth.*

For one thing, the *Zeitgeist,* containing as it does the currently "official" viewpoint, provides a background against which new results can be interpreted. You cannot recognize that something is wrong with the current theory if you are not thoroughly acquainted with what kinds of observations are consistent and inconsistent with it. Beyond that, you are more likely to be disturbed by even a slight discrepancy from theory if you are firmly convinced of the truth of the theory than if you are indifferent to the accepted viewpoint. (Notice that this point is almost opposite to the idea that your commitment to a current viewpoint will lead you to overlook discrepancies.)

Furthermore, the acceptance of an "official viewpoint" gives direction and focus to research. By directing attention to those parts of the conceptual system that are in need of further corroboration, that are vague, or that need further elucidation, an investigator is more apt to come up with significant results. The outcomes will be significant in the sense that they say something meaningful to the majority of scientists in the field who share a common belief system. If the results help to support or to clarify the system, they will be accepted and made part of the body of accepted knowledge. If the results challenge the system, they will eventually have to be dealt with, either by counterevidence, or by additional assumptions added to the system, or by the abandonment of the system.

The last alternative is what Kuhn would call a scientific revolution. It can come about, he feels, only if two conditions hold. The first condition is that as the result of an accumulation of findings that do not directly fit the system, the system has gradually been patched up with supplementary assumptions to help "save it" until it has reached the point of being ridiculously overcomplicated and cumbersome. Such was the situation with the Ptolemaic system at the time Copernicus replaced it with a newer conception that put the sun at the center of the universe. And such was the case recently, at least in the minds of many psychologists, with stimulus-response psychology as its adherents tried to add supplementary hypothesis after supplementary hypothesis to deal with the newer discoveries about instincts, about species

* T. S. Kuhn. *The structure of scientific revolutions.* Chicago: University of Chicago Press, 1962.

differences, about the acquisition of complex learning sets, about the role of curiosity and need for stimulation, and about the nervous system. The second condition is the appearance of a competing system that not only handles the phenomena originally dealt with by the first system, but also can predict new and previously unnoticed phenomena.

CONCLUSIONS ABOUT GETTING IDEAS

Perhaps I have said enough about the origin of ideas to convince you of at least two important features. The first is that we really do not know enough about getting ideas even to speculate wisely about how to encourage fruitful research. The second point is that for almost any suggestion that we might put forth, we can find some advocates of a contradictory approach. With these points as background, I shall conclude this discussion with some comments and observations.

The Role of "Originality" in Psychological Inquiry

Recently there has been a trend towards emphasizing creativity and independent thinking as valuable goals in our educational system. A similar emphasis on encouraging originality has arisen in the teaching of scientific inquiry and especially in the teaching of psychological research. This emphasis, in part, represents a justifiable reaction against overformalization and ritualization in our efforts to teach scientific method to students.

Yet this emphasis may have negative results. For one thing, encouraging "originality" or "being different" for its own sake seems often to result in an unwillingness to tackle currently accepted or standard problems. The young and ambitious psychologist does not want to cover old ground. He wants to innovate, tackle new problems, use new methods, invent new concepts, and attach his name to novel phenomena. Unfortunately, the consequences of such ambition all too frequently are a spate of isolated reports leading nowhere and making contact with neither the past nor the present. Such efforts fly in the face of the fact that the scientific enterprise is a cumulative affair; each new addition to the edifice grows out of, and builds upon, what has already been done.

Emphasis on novelty and rejection of the accepted viewpoints distorts one of the major functions of scientific inquiry. For the value of a scientific investigation does not lie in its novelty. Rather it lies in its additions to our understanding and mastery of the domain under scrutiny. Sometimes such an addition to our knowledge does require new ideas or rejection of the old. But this kind of novelty or revolution is a consequence of the search for a more adequate picture, not the object of the search. In other words, the idea of inquiry is to achieve a better match between our conceptual systems and the phenomena to which they refer; this idea becomes distorted when it is confused with the goal of being "different" or "novel" or "revolutionary."

The Acceptance
of the Current Conceptual Systems

Another potentially harmful consequence of the current emphasis on originality is the possibility that students will no longer be willing to begin their research careers by first mastering and working within a given conceptual system rather than trying to boldly strike out for themselves. Although it is currently fashionable to attack the conservatism and rigidity of old schools of thought in psychology, the most effective research still seems to come from individuals who are loyally dedicated to one of these systems.

Also, most of the so-called revolutions within psychological inquiry came about by men who were "boring from within" rather than from the outside. To bring a change in the prevailing system, one must, it seems, use it as his point of departure. The work of the Würzburg school beginning in 1900 is a case in point. This group, working within the framework of Wundtian structural psychology, saw itself as revolutionary in its decision to apply the accepted methodology of classical introspection to the thought processes. Even though they were breaking with tradition in this step, the psychologists at Würzburg kept almost all the other trappings of the existing school—they started with the accepted notions that only trained introspectionists could supply data, that the data had to be in the form of statements about the basic units of consciousness (sensations, images, and simple feelings), that only conscious events were admissible as psychological data, and that sensations combined according to the laws of association. The revolution they created and the quarrels that resulted when they discovered that some of the elements could not be described by the classic trilogy of sensation-image-feeling eventually resulted in the complete destruction of structuralism and introspection as important forces in contemporary psychology.

The important point to note is that this revolution was not accomplished by a direct challenge to the established order, nor by an attempt to start entirely from scratch. In historical perspective, we can see that it started by clinging to all the essential elements of the Wundtian system, except one. By taking only a little step away from the accepted system, the Würzburgers eventually found that they had helped to destroy the basis of classical psychology and paved the way for *Gestalt* psychology in Europe and behaviorism in the United States.

The Necessity To Be Active
in Empirical Research

Of course it is not sufficient to be immersed in the current *Zeitgeist* of one's chosen field of inquiry. The advance of new ideas and of inquiry comes about through the constant comparison of observations, directly made by the investigator, with expectations drilled into him by his *Zeitgeist*. Concerning this necessity of being continually active in research, F. Bartlett makes this interesting observation: *

It will be found that every first-rate scientific experimenter is also an accurate and eager observer, whether he was one of the early pioneers who first had to rebel against traditional and dogmatic doctrines which got out of touch with facts, or whether, as in these later days, he frequently must make use of the reports of others. Every scientific journal, with whatever branch of knowledge it is concerned, provides plenty of illustrations of workers who show beyond dispute that they know a lot about the reports of others, but who nevertheless achieve no outstanding experimental research of their own. It is still true that merely to hang arguments upon other people's work is not the manner of thinking of the experimental scientist.

The Need for Concentration and Thorough Immersion in the Task

Pavlov dwelt on the problem of just how to tackle psychic secretions for months and months before he decided on his course of action. And then he continually kept changing, improving, and working out his techniques, ideas, and experiments for the remainder of his life. Even when the glimmer of a good idea, or a potentially good idea, comes to an investigator, success seems to follow when he lives with the problem for quite a while, concentrates on it for long periods, turns it over in his mind, and views it from several angles. Only after long and protracted thinking about the problem does the successful investigator feel that he has correctly formulated it. Einstein spent over six years from the time he first asked what happens when an object approaches the speed of light until he finally arrived at what he thought was the correct formulation of the question.

Quite frequently, when a revolutionary idea is finally formulated and exploited, it is recognized as one that has occurred several times previously to the investigator as well as to others. The idea was *there* and available all the time. But now, after much effort and concentration, its significance can be seen as "obvious." In other words, the investigator himself has to keep coming back to an idea before he fully grasps its import.

The Necessity of Exploiting the Idea

It is not enough to "get" a potentially good idea. Before announcing it to the world or before reporting it, an investigator needs to investigate it thoroughly, work out its consequences, and completely master it before rushing into print. Unfortunately, the pressure to publish and the desire to be first often thwarts this obligation. Many investigators find themselves defending ideas or protecting their brainchild under conditions that ought never to have arisen. Pavlov devoted much time, labor, and concentration to the problem before he reported his work on

* F. Bartlett. *Thinking*. London: Allen & Unwin, 1958, p. 113.

the conditioned reflex. Fechner spent ten years between getting his idea and publishing it—during which time he is said to have made 67,072 weight comparisons alone, using himself both as subject and experimenter. Newton and Darwin are just two of many other outstanding examples from the non-psychological sciences.

The Need for Good Ideas

For some reason, the current emphasis on creativity and originality, which may or may not make sense in technology and industry, has spilled over into the area of scientific research. The scientific journals carry articles by authors concerned over the lack of originality and creativity in scientific inquiry. We need new ideas, so they keep telling us. Yet, even a casual reading of the history of inquiry or a contemporary survey of the field of psychology will reveal that there is no shortage of "new" ideas. It is not more ideas that we need. Rather, it is more patient and thorough exploitation and clarification of the ones that we already have. Changes in our thinking and our image of man will not result from our flitting about from idea to idea. Rather, they will come about by our selecting important problems, formulating ideas within these problem areas, and then carefully and thoroughly exploiting these ideas by means of empirical observation.

Getting the Facts

"If the facts used as a basis for reasoning are ill-established or erroneous, everything will crumble or be falsified; and it is thus that errors in scientific theories most often originate in errors of fact." (Claude Bernard, 1865.)

The creative aspect of psychological inquiry, the getting of ideas, does not distinguish it from other creative activities such as literature, art, and invention. What does set psychological and scientific inquiry apart is the manner of gathering, analyzing, and reporting facts. This is another way of saying that scientific inquiry, in addition to being creative, is also *empirical* and *objective*.

32

4

In this chapter I shall spell out some of the implications of the term "empirical" as it applies to scientific inquiry. I shall especially emphasize why the progress of psychology as a science goes hand in hand with the course of its rejection of "facts" that come from everyday forms of observation and experience.

Psychologists' claims to be scientists rest on their ability to accumulate data that conform to the requirements of *objectivity* and *reproducibility*. These twin requirements are captured in the definition of science as "the study of those judgments concerning which universal agreement can be obtained." *
A report of any scientific experiment is, in effect, a recipe, or prescription, telling the reader: "If you look at X under conditions Y you will see Z." Thus, it is taken for granted that, in principle, if anyone wants to repeat your observations, he can follow your instructions and he will "see the same thing" that you reported. Such a prescription immediately rules a large proportion of our experiences out of the domain of science. Many of our personal experiences, many events we have witnessed and are "sure" about, many case histories and anecdotes that form an important part of our belief systems, and many forms of eye-witness accounts that we willingly employ as evidence for important decisions in everyday living—these and much more of the richness of our lives are ruthlessly excluded.

Such stubborn refusal to accept all the "facts" both puzzles and annoys many individuals who want to argue for such things as water divining, astrology, flying saucers, and a host of other belief systems that, in their view, scientists pigheadedly refuse to acknowledge. The scientist seems to be callously indifferent to reports and evidence from a variety of impeccable sources. Instead, he insists that a "fact" is true only if it can be observed under properly specified conditions. Our purpose in this chapter is to point out the reasons for this seemingly cavalier dismissal of nonscientific evidence. To anticipate: We shall find that the development of scientific inquiry can be represented as man's gradual discovery of ways to eliminate the factors that can distort our pictures of the "real world."

THE MAGICIAN VERSUS THE SCIENTIST

In our society, two professional groups that have shown concern about the inadequacies of our perceptual systems are magical entertainers and scientists. The magician's livelihood depends on his ability to exploit the limitations of the human being as an observer. Since the dawn of recorded history, the conjurer has excelled in his practical knowledge of how men observe and register the happenings in the world about them. The scientist, who is a latecomer in the history of mankind, has also made progress by gaining knowledge about the limitations of man as perceiver. Whereas the magician has used

* N. Campbell. *What is science?* New York: Dover, 1952.

his carefully guarded secrets to fool and confound the perceptions of his audiences, the scientist, in his quest for a true picture of the external world, has learned to avoid those kinds of information and situations where observation is most untrustworthy. The scientist seeks to advance knowledge by restricting himself and his colleagues to those kinds of facts on which agreement can be obtained and on which such distorting factors as unconscious wishes, prejudices, and perceptual limitations have least effect.

We can answer part of our question about why the scientist rejects certain kinds of "facts" by describing three different incidents involving magicians. A magician loves nothing better than to put one over on his colleagues. At a convention of magicians, a performer borrowed a deck of playing cards. He then went through the motions of mixing the cards so that face-up cards were interwoven with face-down cards. The onlookers, who were veterans in the art of conjuring, immediately recognized this activity as the well-known "slop-shuffle." They knew that as soon as the shuffle was over the face-up and face-down cards would actually not be interwoven, but would be in two separate packets facing each other. They also knew that the performer's next move would be to secretly turn half of the cards face down so that the entire deck would now be restored to its original condition. This last move, which is known as the "pass," is a very difficult step to accomplish without being detected. In fact, a magician will only perform it under conditions where he can momentarily divert attention away from his hands.

But, on this occasion, the magician made no attempt to cover his moves. In fact, to the surprise of the onlookers the performer made no discernible move at all. Instead, with a flourish, he calmly put the deck on the table and spread it out in a fan, showing that all the cards were facing in the same direction. The magicians immediately began debating among themselves about how the performer had managed to restore the deck to its normal condition right before their eyes. Some claimed that they had seen him actually perform the pass, although they admitted that they had never before seen a magician perform it so fast or skillfully. Others argued that he definitely did not perform the pass, but instead, must have somehow managed to switch decks. This latter suggestion was hooted down on the grounds that it would have involved an even greater feat of legerdemain than performing an invisible pass. The majority of the assembled experts finally concluded that the magician must have employed a trick deck, one in which some of the cards had only backs without faces. Even this latter explanation was not a happy one, because it didn't square with the one "fact" on which everyone could agree—the performer had actually borrowed the cards just before his trick.

At this point the performer, with a triumphant gleam in his eye, proceeded to explain what actually had taken place. The secret was so simple and audacious that it had not occurred to any one of these seasoned magicians. The performer had never mixed the cards in the first place! He did start to go through the motions of the well-known slop-shuffle, but this was pure bluff. Anyone who was at all attentive at this point would have easily seen that after every step the performer simply reversed what he had done. But the magicians, like other human beings, once they thought they "knew" what was taking place, relaxed their guard. They focused all their attention on what was for them the really difficult part of the trick—getting the cards back to their normal condition. It did not occur to anyone present to suspect the possibility that the performer would be bold enough not to mix the cards in the first place!

For a second illustration, let us look at a magician performing before an audience of laymen. He borrows a half-dollar. With the comment that money is being made of cheaper material these days, he calmly proceeds to bend the half-dollar in the middle as if it were made of rubber. The illusion is quite compelling. Yet, all that happens, in addition to the slight suggestion from the magician, is that his fingers slide in and out on the flat surface of the coin as he moves it back and forth in a motion perpendicular to the onlooker. The reason the illusion is so compelling is that this configuration of stimulation is *exactly what would strike the eye if the coin really were bending in the middle.* Whether the onlooker sees fingers sliding back and forth on the surface of a rigid coin or sees a rubbery coin being bent in the middle, depends not on the image hitting the eye but on the context and expectations under which he views this image. If he were a magician who was familiar with this trick, he would see fingers moving on the surface of a rigid coin. If he were an onlooker who has previously been given the appropriate hint, he sees a rubbery coin. Here is a case where two individuals can witness the "same physical happening" and yet "see" two different things.

As our final illustration, let us look in on a show being performed in one of the better night-clubs. The legendary Cardini, dressed in top-hat and tails, is flawlessly performing his beautiful sleight-of-hand feats with cards, balls, and cigarettes. His right hand, immaculately gloved in white, casually reaches out as if to grab something in the air. Slowly he opens his hand and turns it over back and front. Empty, completely empty. Suddenly his monocle drops from his eye and dangles from its string. With his other hand, Cardini calmly reaches down and grasps the monocle, brings it to his mouth, blows some speck of dust off it, then places it back over his eye. Now he returns his gaze to his empty right hand which has apparently been arrested in mid-air during this slight interlude. He reaches out again and, miraculously, his hand displays a full deck of cards spread out in a beautiful fan!

These examples illustrate but three of the principles that magicians have evolved for insuring that their audiences will "see" only what they are supposed to see. In the second example, the magician exploits the fact that our perception typically goes beyond the immediate sensations striking the retina. We automatically "fill in" much of the picture before us by organizing the immediate sensory input in terms of an existing context. In a sense, even at the level of direct observation of "facts," each "fact" depends markedly on our past experience and expectations. You and I can both encounter identical retinal images (or see the same motion picture of an event). You will "see" and report the "fact" that the coin was bent in the middle; I will "see" and report the "fact" that the coin remained rigid while the performer slid his fingers back and forth over its surface.

In the first example, the magician took advantage of the fact that his highly specialized audience shared a common set of expectations. They were quite familiar with the slop-shuffle and it took only a few pretended motions to quickly engage the strong expectation and subsequent "seeing" from all present of the "fact" that the magician performed such a shuffle. It is interesting to speculate that this effect, which completely baffled the magicians, might not have mystified a lay audience at all. They would not be familiar with the trick and its mechanics. Instead of seeing him perform the slop-shuffle, they would have merely seen the magician awkwardly turn a few cards face down and then turn them face up again. Consequently they would not have been puzzled in the least to discover, after this awkward series of maneuvers, that the cards were all facing in the same direction.

The last example brings out still another important principle of deception. The magicians call it "misdirection"; by this they mean the diverting of attention from key manipulations by apparently "normal" incidents. When Cardini's monocle falls from his eye, it is difficult even for those who are familiar with his act to refrain from momentarily diverting their gaze from the right hand to the sudden movement of the monocle. But, for the master magician Cardini, this momentary diversion is all he requires. The right hand, in perfect synchrony with the monocle's fall, can "load up" with cards during this brief interval. And when all eyes return to the previously empty hand, it is hard to realize that it was ever out of sight. In a sense it was not. It was out in the open for all the spectators to watch. Other magicians divert attention by a variety of means such as asking a question and looking directly into the spectator's eyes, or creating a minor, but plausible, diversion, or masking a smaller movement within a larger one.

One more principle of magic is important to emphasize at this point. Among magicians, the rule is "Never repeat the same trick before the same audience or on the same occasion." The rule has a corollary: "Never announce beforehand the precise nature of your trick." Both rules serve the same purpose—to prevent the spectator from knowing precisely where to focus his attention. If an onlooker knows in advance that the magician intends to exchange places with a costumed clown, then he can make sure to watch the magician at all times and note the moment when the performer steps off stage and returns again within a few seconds. Not being forewarned, however, the onlooker will swear, after the act, that the magician never left the stage or his sight during the course of the effect. Given this initial faith in one's observational powers, then, of course, the fact that the magician turns up in the clown's costume while the assistant suddenly is discovered to be wearing the magician's costume, becomes a magic feat which baffles logical explanation.

Of course, the very reason that the magician refuses to repeat a trick is the very reason why the scientist insists on dealing only with those "facts" that can be witnessed and repeated at will. Both the magician and the scientist know the importance of focusing attention on key aspects of an event *before* the event occurs. A scientific "fact," under these terms, is one that comes with a specification of the conditions and procedure for viewing it. If the event, like the magic trick, is a unique historical incident that cannot be repeated for others to observe, then the event has no status as a scientific fact. The facts of science have nothing to do with particular and unique occurrences. Instead, the facts of science are just those events that different observers at different places and times, when following the accompanying prescription, can experience in the same terms.

REASONS WHY NONSCIENTIFIC OBSERVATIONS ARE NOT ACCEPTABLE

We have looked at only a few possible factors affecting the outcome of an observation. Here we shall consider more systematically factors that lead to distortion of observations. In doing so we shall borrow examples both from nonscientific and from scientific situations. Such illustrations will make the point that even a scientist, in scientific activities, is fallible as a perceiver. And this should not surprise us. The scientist is, after all, a human being with the same afflictions of pride, emotion, prejudice, enthusiasm, and sensory limitation that beset us all. The illustrations will also serve to remind us that the goal of objective observation is an ideal rather than a reality. Scientific observation does not differ from everyday observation by being infallible, although it is quantitatively less fallible than ordinary observation. Rather, it differs from everyday observation in that the scientist gradually uncovers his previous errors and corrects them; and he uses the example of these errors to improve his observational procedures and to build in new safeguards against future repetition of distortion. Indeed, the history of psychology as a science has been the development of procedural and instrumental aids that gradually eliminate or correct for biases and distortions in making observations.

The Limits of Sensory Discrimination

One of the chief values of instrumentation in science is the increase in range it gives to the scientist's observational powers. Another advantage comes from the substitution of a more reliable and objective judgment for an inconsistent and subjective one. It is much easier to obtain agreement on pointer readings than it is to get different observers to agree whether a subject shows "anxiety" or not. Where observation involves poor viewing conditions or fine discriminations on the part of the observer, distortions of judgment are especially likely to occur. A particularly tragic example is the case of the so-called *n-rays*.

The n-ray was discovered in 1902 by the eminent French physicist M. Blondlot. The discovery was confirmed and extended by other French scientists. In the year 1904 alone, there appeared 77 different scientific publications devoted to the n-ray. Controversy over the n-ray quickly arose when it was realized that German, Italian, and American physicists could not duplicate Blondlot's findings. The n-ray, it seemed, could be observed only on French soil. Eventually, the American physicist R. W. Wood, who had unsuccessfully attempted to duplicate n-rays in his own laboratory at Johns Hopkins, visited Blondlot in Nancy. Wood's own encounter with Blondlot is best described in his own words.

He first showed me a card on which some circles had been painted in luminous paint. He turned down the gas light and called my attention to their increased luminosity when the n-ray was turned on. I said I saw no change. He said that was because my eyes were not sensitive enough, so that proved nothing. I asked him if I could move an opaque lead screen in and out of the path of the rays while he called out the fluctuations on the screen. He was almost 100% wrong and called out fluctuations when I made no movement at all, and that proved a lot, but I held my tongue.

Wood conducted other tests which clearly demonstrated that the n-rays existed only in Blondlot's imagination. By 1909 there were no more publications involving the n-ray. Blondlot himself never recovered from this incident and died in disgrace.*

Frameworks within Which
"Observations" Are Interpreted

As we have shown, the same events can be "seen" as different "facts" when two observers bring different frames of reference to the situation. The case of the n-rays illustrates their difficulty in addition to the difficulties of observation near the sensory threshold. Listen to what the physiologist W. B. Carpenter had to say in 1877: †

The two different modes in which Spiritualists and their opponents view the same facts, according to their respective predispositions, is well brought out in cases of the so-called "materialization"—a party being assembled in a front drawing-room, the "medium" retires into a backroom separated from it by curtains, and professes there to go into a trance. After a short interval, during which the lights are turned down so as to make "darkness visible," a figure dressed in some strange guise enters between the curtains, and displays itself to the spectators as an "embodied spirit." Precluded from any direct interference with the performance, a sceptic among the audience slyly puts some ink on his fingers, and whilst this is still wet, grasps the "spirit-hand," which he finds very like a mortal one. The

* See also E. Z. Vogt and R. Hyman. *Water witching U.S.A.* Chicago: University of Chicago Press, 1959.
† W. B. Carpenter. *Mesmerism, spiritualism, &c.* New York: Appleton, 1877, pp. vii-viii.

"spirit" withdraws behind the curtains, after a short interval the lights are raised, and the "medium" returns to the company *in propria persona*. The sceptic then points out inkstains on one of the "medium's" hands, and tells what he has done.

These are the *facts* of the case. Now, the "common-sense" interpretation of these facts is, that the "medium" is a cheat, and the "embodied spirit" a vulgar ghost personated by him; and until adequate proof shall have been given to the contrary, I maintain that we are perfectly justified in holding to this interpretation, confirmed as it is by the exposure of the trick in every instance in which adequate means have been taken for its detection. But the explanation of his inked fingers given by the "medium" is, that the impress made on the hand of the "embodied spirit" has been transferred "according to a well-known law of Spiritualism" to his own; and this assumption is regarded as more probable, by such as have accepted the system, than that their pet "medium" is a cheat, and their belief in him a delusion.

The Aspects Attended To

In the area of selective attention, psychologists have demonstrated over and over again the limitations of the human being as an eyewitness. F. K. Berrien describes a demonstration of a type that has been done before many audiences under a variety of circumstances with the same outcome: *

A great many informal classroom experiments have demonstrated the influence of attention and expectation on subsequent recall. For example, the author arranged to have a student walk into the class late and interrupt the lecture by a declaration of having lost some white rats. He walked slowly across the room in front of the class, turned around, and went out, all the while carrying on a previously rehearsed conversation with the instructor concerning the loss of, and search for, the rats. In spite of the fact that the student-actor was well known to the class, estimates of his weight ranged from 145 to 210 (actual weight 190); eight of the forty-three students declared he wore a maroon-colored sweater (actually he wore a gray-tan, double-breasted coat); and a majority declared vehemently he searched in the corners looking for his rats (he made one furtive glance toward the corner of the room contrary to instructions to keep his eyes on the instructor). The reports on the sweater and his searching were at least partly due to expectation, the prevailing color of sweaters on this particular campus being maroon, while the searching was expected in view of the conversation.

Even under conditions where the observers know that they will be immediately tested for the accuracy of what they are going to witness, such distortions inevitably take place. No wonder, then, that the scientist has learned to be skeptical about data from casual observation. The psychologist, in particular, knows quite well how his own and others' observations can be misleading. He has learned to trust neither his own reports nor those of others—unless these reports are accompanied by clear specification of how anyone else might check the same facts if he so desires. This clear specification must include a statement of the relevant conditions, what is to be looked for, what is to be done, and how it is to be recorded.

* F. K. Berrien. *Practical psychology*. Rev. ed. New York: Macmillan, 1952, pp. 482–483.

Self-deception

Other studies on memory, rumor transmission, and personality have demonstrated the variety of ways in which our perceptions and reports can be influenced and distorted by such personal factors as values, motivation, prior expectations, social norms, and the like. In the area of self-deception comes a variety of phenomena that occur because an individual has poor feedback from his muscles. Tables can seemingly move of their own accord, divining rods dip, the ouija board spell out a message—all such things can occur because, without adequate feedback from our muscles, we can unwittingly respond to our subconscious expectations and move objects in such a way that we are convinced that the objects are self-propelled.*

The psychologist as a scientist, then, rejects many sources of observations —of his own as well as of others. He knows that man is a highly fallible observer. Despite the best intentions the human onlooker is limited by the sensitivity of his perceptual apparatus, by the frameworks and categories he has for ordering his perceptual experience, by the limited span of things he can attend to at any one time, and by motivational and physiological aspects that lead to self-deception. The growth of psychology as a science goes hand in hand with the gradual discovery and elimination of these human defects in the gathering of data.

PSYCHOLOGICAL INQUIRY AND ACCEPTABILITY OF OBSERVATIONS

The development of psychology as a science has paralleled changes in the standards of what observations are permissible. When Wundt founded experimental psychology in 1879, the fundamental source of data for psychology was to be the observations made by trained introspectionists upon the contents of their own consciousness. So long as the trained observers operated under Wundt's supervision and on simple sensory inputs, no one questioned the scientific status of these data. Apparently two different observers could describe the same stimulus in similar sensory terminology. Although the protocols from such research made dull reading, the belief was unquestioned that they represented scientific observation.

The most crushing blow to this reliance on introspective data came some 25 years after the founding of Wundt's laboratory. Psychologists at the University of Würzburg began a series of studies on thinking. Immediately they encountered difficulties in applying the introspective method. For one thing, their observers reported some elements that did not correspond to the classic elements of sensation, image, and simple feelings. The new and indescribable

* For a detailed discussion of self-deception, see Vogt and Hyman, *ibid.*

conscious elements were eventually called "imageless thoughts." In this country, Titchener, the leading exponent of Wundtian psychology took issue with the Würzburg school. He said they were mistaken in reporting these imageless thoughts. The existence of such entities was more a matter of poor introspective technique than empirical "fact." A controversy raged with Wundt and Titchener on one side and the Würzburg psychologists on the other side. The controversy demonstrated, at least for subsequent psychologists, that introspection was not a reliable tool for the gathering of scientific data. What an introspectionist reported seemed to be as much a matter of his training and the laboratory in which he functioned as it was a matter of observing repeatable and "objective" facts.

We have seen how Pavlov also found introspective and subjective data unreliable and untrustworthy. At first, as he himself informs us, he attempted, with his colleagues, to put himself in the place of the dog—to reproduce by imagination the animal's probable feelings, expectations, desires, and such, as he reacted to a stimulus that signalled food. Again and again, in different lectures, Pavlov tells us of his struggle to find a system or method for interpreting the conditioned reflex.*

But how is this to be studied? Taking the dog when he eats rapidly, snatches something in his mouth, chews for a long time, it seems clear that at such a time the animal strongly desires to eat, and so he rushes to the food, seizes it, and falls to eating. He longs to eat. Another time the movements are slower, less avid, and therefore we say the dog does not want so strongly to eat. When he eats, you see the work of the muscles alone, striving in every way to seize the food in the mouth, to chew and to swallow it. From all this we can say that he derives pleasure from it. When on the contrary an inedible substance happens to get into the mouth, and the dog ejects it, spews it out with the tongue, shakes his head, then we involuntarily want to say that this is unpleasant for the animal. Now when we proceeded to explain and analyse this, we readily adopted this trite point of view. We had to deal with the feelings, wishes, conceptions, etc., of our animal. The results were astounding, extraordinary; I and one of my colleagues came to irreconcilable opinions. We could not agree, could not prove to one another which was right. For some decades before, and also afterwards, we could settle all our questions, we are able to decide one way or another, and the dissension ended.

After this we had to deliberate carefully. It seemed probable that we were not on the right track. The more we thought about the matter, the greater grew our conviction that it was necessary to choose another exit. The first steps were very difficult, but along the way of persistent, tense and concentrated thinking I finally reached the firm ground of pure objectivity. We absolutely prohibited ourselves (in the laboratory there was an actual fine imposed) the use of such psychological expressions as the dog guessed, wanted, wished, etc.

What Pavlov found "astounding" and "extraordinary" was the fact that two experimenters dealing with the same experimental situation could report different "facts." As he puts it in the preface to his book: †

* I. P. Pavlov. *Lectures on conditioned reflexes.* New York: International Publishers, 1963, pp. 263–264. By permission of International Publishers Co., Inc.
   † *Ibid.,* p. 38.

We were now brought face to face with a situation which had no precedent in our laboratory. In our explanation of this internal world we diverged in two opposite paths. New experiments did not bring us into agreement nor produce conclusive results, and this in spite of the usual laboratory custom, according to which new experiments undertaken by mutual consent are generally decisive.

Pavlov finally traced what was wrong to the language and concepts that he and his colleagues were employing to describe the dog's behavior. When they had studied the digestive processes in physiological terms, they had never encountered disagreement about what the "facts" of each experiment were. This was because they had used the "objective" approach. They did not talk about the feelings or consciousness of the dog. Rather, they talked about the stimulation of the receptors in the mouth by the chemical properties of the food, the neural transmission of this stimulation via the central nervous system to the efferent nerves, and the activation of the digestive glands by these nerves. In this context, they observed what they placed in the dog's mouth (the stimulus) and the output of the appropriate digestive glands (the response). When the scientists confined their observations to such observable data, there were no disagreements about what happened. Different observers could witness and report the same thing.

Pavlov's big insight, one that had already been suggested by Sechenov, was to treat psychic secretion as a reflex that operates according to the same principles as the reflexes he had studied in the earlier work in digestion. It took him some time to realize that this insight implied that he could use the same objective approach and language to handle this problem. When he finally decided to employ the "objective" approach—to describe each experiment in terms of the stimulus (the bell, the food, their time relationships) and the response (the output of the salivary glands) instead of the conscious state of the dog—he found that he achieved that consensus among observers that was essential to scientific observation. Once he had achieved a method for dealing with conditioned reflexes under conditions where he and his co-workers could observe and report the same "facts," then he knew he had a problem that could be tackled within the accepted limits of science.

THE CONCEPT OF "CONTROL" IN SCIENTIFIC OBSERVATION

We have taken pains to get across the reasons why several classes of "evidence" cannot qualify as scientific knowledge. We should also discuss what kinds of observation do qualify as scientific data. In general, all scientific data are based on controlled observation. Our task is now to examine what we mean by "control" in this context and to illustrate the different implications of the term with some examples from psychological inquiry.

Psychological inquiry is *controlled* inquiry. This means, among other things, that observations are made in terms of a *conceptual focus;* the data are gathered in such a way as to be pertinent to a more or less restricted issue.

The scientist succeeds in his inquiry only to the extent that he can restrict his attention to those aspects of his investigation that will be pertinent to the questions he has raised. The conceptual focus helps the investigator to *select* from the myriad of possibilities just those features that convey relevant information.

In addition to a focus, the observations are made under explicitly *specified* conditions. The results of scientific observation are accompanied with a specification of what was sought, under what conditions, and by what procedures. This specification also acts as a *prescription;* it tells other members of the scientific community how they might check or repeat the reported observations. It specifies what to look for, how to look for it, under what conditions, with what means.

The key feature of psychological inquiry, as revealed in the word "control," lies in the constraints that are built into the observational situation. Methods of gathering data differ in the constraints that are explicitly placed on the investigator. The procedure might constrain the observer in terms of what he looks at, how he looks, and what he records. The methods also differ in their constraints on the conditions under which the observations are made— the possible background stimulation, the foreground stimulation, or both. Finally, the methods differ in the constraints, if any, they impose on the subject; the procedures might entail constraining extraneous and incidental responses, the form of the responses that form the data, or both.

We can use this breakdown of the locus of constraints—in the observer, in the environment, in the subject—for a brief discussion of another breakdown of techniques for gathering data. A popular classification of such procedures is this triad: naturalistic studies, differential studies, and experiments.

NATURALISTIC STUDIES

Generally, naturalistic observation is an attempt to look at behavior of organisms in their natural state. The investigator tries to interfere as little as possible with the behavior of his subjects in the process of gathering data. The ethologists, who attempt to watch and record the behavior of animals in their natural habitat, belong here. The recent study by Leon Festinger and his colleagues on a group that was awaiting the end of the world is another example.*

These investigators were looking for a real-life situation in which an expectation could definitely be contradicted. They discovered and infiltrated a group whose members believed that the world would come to an end on a specified day. The investigators wanted to observe the behavior leading up to the designated day and they wanted to be around to record the behavior

* L. Festinger, H. W. Riecken, and S. Schachter. *When prophecy fails.* Minneapolis: University of Minnesota Press, 1956.

of the members when the expected day of judgment did not materialize. The success of their observations depended on their skill in becoming accepted members of the group, in observing and recording what happened, and in not influencing the behavior of the individuals in the group by their presence.

Piaget's Clinical Method

A variant of the naturalistic method is sometimes called the clinical method, so named because the data often arise from observations made by a therapist in the course of interviewing and treating his patients for psychological problems. This was the method employed by Freud for the observations that led to his theory of psychoanalysis. The Swiss psychologist Jean Piaget also calls his method of observation "the clinical method." Piaget's studies are frequently preceded by naturalistic observations of children in various settings. From these naturalistic observations he devises test situations and questions with which to confront the child.

Here is an example of Piaget's procedure. The experimenter confronts children of various ages with the following demonstration: He clasps his hands, and by repeatedly pressing his palms together he produces a small current of air which usually takes the child by surprise. The experimenter then asks the child about the origin of this air. An exchange between a six-and-a-half-year-old boy and the experimenter went as follows:*

Experimenter:	What am I doing?
Child:	You are clapping.
Experimenter:	What do you hear?
Child:	A slap.
Experimenter:	What is it?
Child:	The hands.
Experimenter:	What are the hands doing?
Child:	They are clapping and that makes it blow.
Experimenter:	What is blowing?
Child:	Wind.
Experimenter:	Where does the wind come from?
Child:	From the hands.
Experimenter:	And the wind of the hands?
Child:	From inside the skin.
Experimenter:	Where from?
Child:	From the meat inside.
Experimenter:	Where is this wind?
Child:	All through the body.

Piaget's method emphasizes flexibility and the avoidance of constraining the child's natural thought processes. Therefore Piaget does not concern himself with standardizing his tasks or questions. No two children are ever exposed to the identical sequence of tasks or questions.

* J. Piaget. *The child's conception of physical causality.* Paterson, N. J.: Littlefield, Adams, 1960.

The emphasis of naturalistic and clinical observation, as can be seen from these examples, is to place minimal constraints on nature while observing her. The ideal is to look at behavior as it naturally occurs. Deliberate intervention by experimental manipulation or standardized tests is avoided because such unnatural interruptions of ongoing behavior might distort and alter the behavior to such an extent that it destroys its relevance. J. H. Flavell explains Piaget's defense of his procedure in these terms: *

Piaget feels that only through such a method can one get to the heart of the child's cognitive structure and describe it as it really is. One simply must adopt a technique, whatever its hazards and difficulties, which permits the child to move on his own intellectually, to display the cognitive orientation which is natural to him at that period in his development.

Advantages and Disadvantages of Naturalistic Observation

The advantages of Piaget's approach are also its disadvantages from the point of view of scientific observation. Because naturalistic and clinical methods avoid placing constraints on what they observe, they produce data that are difficult to reproduce and that typically violate our standards of specificity and standardization of observational procedure. Because no two children are ever treated identically by Piaget or his colleagues, it becomes impossible to separate differences produced by the method of inquiry from actual differences in the psychological viewpoint of the child. Heavy reliance is placed on the skill and ingenuity of the interviewer in asking questions, in following the child's line of reasoning, and in interacting with him. Some observers will have much better success than others, but it will be impossible to specify why. Without elaborate precautions it also becomes impossible for an experimenter to avoid putting words and thoughts into a child's replies by the questions he asks and by the things he focuses his attention upon.

Because the data emerging from naturalistic observation fail to meet the standards of scientific objectivity, the research of Piaget, until recently, was ignored by American psychologists. Undeterred by the criticisms of his observational procedures by American psychologists, Piaget and his colleagues in Geneva have carried out their work for more than 40 years, gradually building up an elaborate body of knowledge and theory about the development of thought structures from infancy to adulthood. Recently, however, American psychologists have begun to pay attention to Piaget's work. The theories and results have been found to fit well into the current climate of discovery and theoretical development of American psychology. In many remarkable ways his work has been found to anticipate or parallel the work being done in this country on complex learning in monkeys, the formation

* J. H. Flavell. *The developmental psychology of Jean Piaget.* Princeton: Van Nostrand, 1963.

and organization of concepts, and the motivational properties of discrepancies from one's expectations.

We come to an interesting paradox. Contemporary psychological research is now heavily influenced by the work of two outstanding figures—Sigmund Freud and Jean Piaget. Both of these men based their major conclusions and theories squarely on data which they obtained by the clinical method. Both of these men have produced ideas and concepts that now guide many different investigations into the motivational and thinking processes of children and adults. Yet, much of the work and data produced by these men was, and still is, rejected as lying outside the scope of scientific observation. By no stretch of the imagination can we attribute the qualities of specificity, reproducibility, objectivity, or standardization to their data.

The solution to this paradox lies in both the distinction between early and late stages of a scientific inquiry, and in the role that different observational procedures can play in facilitating other phases of the research process. Both Freud and Piaget make their impact on contemporary research not in terms of methodology but in terms of conceptualizations they devised from which we can begin a systematic inquiry. Their work belongs to the "natural history" stage of inquiry—the beginnings of inquiry, when the first task is to get a feel for what is going on and what the important concepts and questions might be.

Naturalistic and clinical observation are more closely allied with the phase of *getting ideas* than they are with the phase of *interpreting* or evaluating the ideas. In getting ideas, in formulating the problem within a new domain, it is important not to impose constraints prematurely. Both Freud and Piaget tried to gather data under conditions where they would not place too many constraints on what could take place. They were trying to see and describe behavior as it actually exists in a given cultural setting. Such clinical observation does not produce the kind of data on which consensus can easily be obtained. Such data depend intimately on the powers and observational skills of the observer. And such skills, in turn, do not belong to scientific inquiry because they cannot be specified and objectified.

Such observations, then, can be very important for originating and setting up problems for later stages of inquiry. The very feature that makes such observational procedures inadequate for providing scientific data probably accounts for their success in raising questions and providing creative ideas for guiding later inquiry. The success of such observation, then, depends not on the specific data it produces, but rather on the questions it raises. It is when we start gathering facts specifically oriented to answering these questions that we provide data for the scientific body of knowledge. For later stages of research and for evaluating questions raised by earlier stages, then, we have to employ observational procedures that are more standardized and that place more constraints on what can be observed.

The kinds of observational procedures that come under the heading of differential methods typically employ existing variations as a way of classifying data. If we want to study the effect of sex upon problem-solving, for example, we take a sample of boys and girls, equated for age and intelligence, and observe the differences in performance between the two groups. The independent variable in such an investigation, sex, is a difference already existing in nature before the investigator came upon the scene. All the differential methods, as distinct from the experimental methods, exploit differences that already exist rather than differences that are deliberately created by the investigator. Sometimes the differences are in terms of qualitative categories, such as male and female, Negro and white, social class, psychiatric diagnosis, and so forth. Frequently, the differences are in terms of where the individuals are located on some underlying dimension as determined by scores on an aptitude test, an achievement test, or an attitude scale.

An observation results in the classification of an individual or group in terms of at least two principles of classification. Piaget's investigations actually straddle both the clinical and the differential methods in this respect. For he uses his clinical method to make some judgment about the structure of a child's thinking process. He then attempts to see how the variations in thought structure correlate with the chronological age of the child.

For example, in the illustrative protocol from one of Piaget's experiments we saw the experimenter asking the child where the air comes from when he presses his hands together. Children below the age of six years respond as if they believe that the hands produce air by drawing upon the supply of air outside of the room. Children at age seven see the air as coming out of the experimenter's body. It is not until the child is nine that he supplies a correct explanation—the hands operate on the air already in the room.

This attempt to collect data on thought processes as a function of age is one example of the differential method. The reason we tend to classify Piaget's procedure more under the clinical than the differential label is that his method does not allow us to reproduce and check his observations objectively. His data cannot be used to quantify outcomes, to indicate the variation of performance at different age levels, and so on. Instead, we designate as "differential" only those procedures wherein the data are collected in such a way that we can specify and standardize the observational procedure for classifying the subject (in this case a child) according to two or more principles (in this case, age and level of thought product).

A more appropriate illustration of the differential method as it is applied to Piaget's problem is illustrated in a study of Jacqueline Goodnow's.* Among

* Jacqueline Goodnow. A test of milieu effects with some of Piaget's tasks. *Psychol. Monogr.,* 1962, 76, Whole number 555.

the tasks she employed were judgments of weight, volume, and space. Although these tasks were all adopted from similar ones employed by Piaget, Goodnow standardized the tasks so that a set of instructions and materials were presented in identical fashion to all the children in her investigation. In this way, Goodnow can present, along with her data, the explicit tasks and instructions she employed, so that anyone who wants to repeat her study can do so, being confident that at least the tasks employed are the same in both studies. For example, Goodnow describes the procedure for the judgment of weight as follows:

The experimenter takes two round balls of clay about the size of a large walnut. He says: "I am going to weigh these first just to check that they're the same. You know that when this needle is straight up or *almost* straight, the two pieces weigh the same." With the two pieces on the two sides of the balance, the experimenter asks: "Weigh the same?" If the subject shows much hesitation or says "no," the experimenter adds: "Are they almost the same? A little bit different doesn't matter in this game."

When the subject agrees that the two pieces are equal in weight, the experimenter says, "Now I take one piece and make it like this [press one piece flat into a pancake shape]. Now if I put the two pieces on the scale again, would they weigh the same or would one be heavier than the other?"

The experimenter then asks: "Which one would be heavier (if appropriate)? Can you tell me why?" If the subject "can't say why," the experimenter takes a small piece away from the flat-shaped clay and asks again.

Goodnow presents similarly detailed instructions for the other tasks. The judgment of volume required the subject to first judge whether two jugs of water contained the same amount; then to judge whether the height of water rose the same amount in the jugs when clay balls of same shape and weight were put into them; and finally to predict if the water would rise to the same height if the clay balls were of same weight but of different shape. The judgment of space required the subject to estimate whether the same amount of grass was available for grazing when 12 houses were dispersed over the field rather than concentrated in one part of the same field.

Although these procedures still do not have the same degree of standardization as does an accepted intelligence test, they represent a big step towards bringing Piaget's tasks into the domain of scientific observation. In Piaget's version of the judgment of weight task, for example, we are never sure just how the task was presented to child, in what order the questions were asked, and so on. In Goodnow's adaptation we not only have a reasonably clear idea of just how the experimenter treated each subject, but we also can attempt to repeat her study with some assurance that we are presenting the tasks and collecting our data in much the same manner as did Goodnow.

As one part of a larger study, Goodnow wanted to see if the performance on these tasks followed the same order of relationship to age that Piaget has reported. She found, in agreement with Piaget, that children are able to show conservation of weight at an earlier age than they can demonstrate conservation of volume. Unfortunately for the complete support of Piaget's observations, the performance on the spatial task did not follow the predicted ordering; this task turned out to be as difficult as was the task on judgment of volume, although it was predicted to be the easiest to master.

Goodnow indicates some possible reasons why the results on conservation of space do not fit the outcome one would predict from Piaget's work. And this discussion reveals both the advantages and disadvantages of employing standardized procedures for obtaining observations. Goodnow, for the sake of getting reproducible, scientific data, had to observe each subject under as nearly identical conditions as possible. Piaget and his colleagues, however, adapt the task for each child and his age-level. At Geneva, a child sometimes is allowed to start with a simpler task and work his way up to the more complicated judgment. Only the oldest children in Piaget's studies begin directly with the task as employed by Goodnow. Thus, from Piaget's data we cannot tell how much of the early mastery of the space task is due to actual conservation of space, how much is due to the skill of interviewer in leading the child gradually into the task, and how much is due to the use of different tasks at different ages. Piaget's procedure thus confounds the job of comparing performances within age levels, across age levels, and across different studies. Yet, without his flexible procedure, Piaget may have missed seeing that with the proper build-up a child can actually master the space task. Again, we see that Piaget's procedure is best fitted, when in the hands of a master observer, for obtaining leads to new phenomena and getting a feel for what types of concepts best describe children's thought structures. But when we want to confirm or test Piaget's ideas, the use of observations from his clinical method can only lead to argument and confusion.

The Correlational Method

Unquestionably, the most frequently employed method of observation in the field of psychology is the correlational method, a particularly tempting approach to the collection of data. The term "the correlational method" frequently refers to a specific method of testing for relationships between two variables. But as we employ the term here, it will refer to all methods that seek to find a relationship between two or more variables as they exist in nature. A typical approach is to divide a collection of individuals into two groups on the basis of some variable of theoretical or practical interest. Some recent favorites among these dichotomies are authoritarian versus equalitarian, conformist versus nonconformist, original versus less original, intelligent versus less intelligent, leveling versus sharpening, high versus low in need for achievement, and rigid versus flexible. The variable of interest is usually called the "dependent variable," while other variables that are employed to characterize or predict a subject's standing on this dependent variable are typically called "independent variables." In correlational studies the choice of dependent and independent variables is somewhat arbitrary. Usually the choice reflects the direction in which the investigator considers the cause-effect relationship. The "cause" becomes the independent variable, the "effect" the dependent variable.

One example of a correlational study is an investigation of creativity in architects.* On the basis of nominations by editors of architectural magazines and members of the architectural faculty at the University of California, a group of 40 of the "most creative" architects in the United States was invited to spend three days at the University of California at Berkeley. During their stay, the creative architects were observed, rated, interviewed, and tested— the results of this systematic assessment procedure yielded 1000 different measures for each man. The measures reflected such things as interests, attitudes, preferences, values, intellectual performance, abilities, and a variety of other measures that can be obtained from a large battery of psychological tests and assessment procedures. Two other groups of "less creative" architects were chosen to serve as comparison groups. The data from the individuals in these latter two groups were collected by means of questionnaires and tests that were mailed to these individuals at their residences.

This procedure resulted in the following types of data from each individual in the study. Each man was classified according to a criterion or dependent variable as either "creative" or "less creative"; secondly, each man was classified or assigned a position on 1000 different predictors, or independent variables. The goal of the procedure, of course, was to find independent variables that would be related to the creative classifications. Such a study must deal with many problems. On this particular study we can raise some questions about the equivalence of the measurement situation—the creative architects were observed while on the campus and in the presence of the investigators whereas the comparison groups supplied data on themselves by filling out test and questionnaire forms in the privacy of their offices or homes. More important and relevant to all correlational studies is the problem of explaining or accounting for the relationships that are actually obtained. Does the fact that the creative architects score high on theoretical and esthetic values indicate that the creative architects are also characterized by other interests and background that go along with this value system? Would such a value system also be found among young architects who will be recognized as creative in the future? Does the greater display of self-confidence by the more creative architects indicate that self-confidence is an essential or contributory factor in making one creative, or is self-confidence the fruit of having "arrived" and being universally acknowledged as "successful"?

Another difficulty with the correlational approach, is the tendency to commit the "ecological fallacy"—to attribute to each individual the pattern of traits that characterizes the group as a whole. It is all too easy to lapse into a discussion of "the creative person" on the basis of results that differentiate one group from another. And yet, these differences might be useful

* D. W. MacKinnon. The nature and nurture of creative talent. *Amer. Psychol.*, 1962, 17, 484–495.

in distinguishing groups of individuals from each other and still fail to characterize any particular individual as such.

Despite these and many other difficulties that confront the user of the differential methods, when they are employed in conjunction with other methods and within a conceptual framework that eschews haphazardly trying any combination of variables until you find one that "works," these methods can effectively add to our knowledge. The methods find their greatest scope in helping us to probe into questions where experimentation is difficult or impossible. Areas where differential methods have been most effective include studies of abilities and work performance, opinion changes, the effects of mass media, voting behavior, shifts in attitudes and opinions of large groups of individuals, the sample surveys, and the large-scale interview studies. The differential methods have proven their worth by adding many valuable ideas and providing a bridge between natural settings and smaller-scale laboratory studies in artificial settings.

THE EXPERIMENTAL METHODS

Many of the differential methods and all of the experimental methods involve *induced responses;* an investigator introduces a standard stimulus or does something and then observes what a subject does in response to this stimulus. In the differential methods, responses are not induced when the data are ratings and biographies that can be obtained without directly involving the subject being observed. But when the investigator asks the subject to respond to a standardized test or to an interview question or has him perform on a standardized task for the purpose of classifying him in terms of some dependent or independent variable, then he is deliberately inducing responses for the purpose of obtaining data.

What, then, distinguishes the experimental methods from the differential methods? The essential difference lies in the experimenter's *control* over the independent variable. In experimental investigations the experimenter actually manipulates the independent variable. He then can observe changes in the dependent variable that follow upon the values of the independent variable. In the study on creative architects, the investigator could not arbitrarily manipulate the variable of "creativity"—a man was either "creative" or "less creative" on the basis of factors that were beyond the psychologist's control. But when an experimenter wants to study the effect of hours without eating on a rat's speed in running down an alleyway to get food, he can control which rats are deprived for one hour, 24 hours, or whatever values he selects, and he can control which rats form the baseline, or comparison, group. This additional source of control on the part of the experimenter gives him a power the user of differential methods lacks. The experimenter can either match the rats in each group so that they are comparable in other variables that the experimenter wishes to exclude or he can balance out these irrelevant factors by randomly assigning rats to each condition. Depending on the study, the experimenter might even use each rat as its own baseline by comparing its performances under experimental and control treatments. He can observe the same rat after it has been deprived for one hour, again when it has been deprived for 24 hours, and so on.

The various problems, advantages, and disadvantages that go into assigning individuals different values of the independent variable, as well as the problem of whether to have each individual perform under each value of the independent variable or only under one condition—these are issues included under the heading of "design of experiments." Courses and books that go under this title are generally treated as a branch of applied statistics. Considering various available designs usually involves questions of how much information can be obtained per unit of observation, how many variables are worth studying simultaneously, whether matching or randomizing is the better strategy, and the number of observations that should be made.

Although we cannot elaborate here on the many different designs that can and are employed in experimental psychology, we can illustrate the basic principle of all experimentation. In essence, the idea is to do something to an individual and observe his reaction under conditions where his performance can be measured against a known baseline. Ideally, the baseline is the behavior we would have observed had we not done "something" to the subject. For example, as part of larger study on communication and persuasion, Carl I. Hovland and his colleagues tested the proposition that active participation in delivering a communication will lead to readier acceptance of it than would passive listening to the same communication.* One communication was to the effect that television will result in the closing of two out of every three movie theaters within the next three years. The experimental subjects were given a prepared outline of this communication and then were asked to deliver an informal talk to the other subjects based on this outline; during the delivery of this talk each subject was asked to play the role of a sincere advocate of the position he was describing. The investigators wanted to know if role-playing activity had any measurable effect on the subject's previously expressed opinion. They found that 45 per cent of the active participants showed "sizable" changes in their opinion towards believing that the movie theaters would shut down within the next three years.

Now, in order to attribute this change to the fact of active participation, the experimenters need to have a baseline which indicates how much change to expect from comparable individuals who are exposed to the same information but who otherwise do not actively try to communicate it. In other words, they have to know how individuals would respond who are comparable and who are treated the same way in every respect except on the independent variable. Fortunately, the experimental method enabled the investigators to arrange for such a comparison. The "passive" controls consisted of subjects

* C. I. Hovland, I. L. Janis, and H. H. Kelley. *Communication and persuasion.* New Haven: Yale University Press, 1953.

from the same pool of students who read the same communication and who listened to the oral presentations of the active participants. Of these subjects only 21 per cent showed a sizable increment in favor of the communication. This baseline, which is less than half the percentage of active participants who showed considerable change, supplied the experimenters with a gauge by which they could judge the extent to which the observed effect could be attributed to the independent variable.

Some of the most effective psychological research combines the experimental with the differential approach. A typical experiment, for example, might use a differential variable such as sex to separate subjects into two groups—male and female. And then the experimenters might randomly assign each subject within a group to one of the experimental classifications, or "treatments." For example, half the subjects of each sex might be asked to perform a task under "stress" conditions and the remaining subjects might be asked to perform the same task under "relaxed" conditions. The experimenter could then see whether stress and relaxation had the same effect within both groups or whether stress differs from relaxation depending on the sex of the subject. When the effects of one experimental variable depend on how the subject is classified on another independent variable, the experimenter calls this an "interaction effect"—the effects of sex and stress, say, would interact if the same stress that disrupted performance in females facilitated performance in males. There would be no interaction between sex and stress if the effects were identical in both groups—if stress disrupted performance of both boys and girls to the same extent.

An example of an interaction between a differential and an experimental variable can be illustrated by an investigation of the effects of language on perception in children. In a series of studies that somewhat parallel the work of Piaget on the development of thinking in children, Russian psychologists have been studying how perceptual and language behavior develop with age. Although the Russians use the differential approach in their search for correlates of age in children, they go beyond Piaget in supplementing the differential studies with experiments in which they try to alter the age at which certain effects will occur. This emphasis on the experimental approach to children's behavior almost certainly stems from the Russians' efforts to pattern their methods after the work of Pavlov, the founder of Russian psychology.

In one study the experimenter shows a child two cards. One card contains a red circle on a grey background (RED-grey); the other has a green circle on a yellow background (GREEN-yellow). The child is told to squeeze a ball with his right hand whenever the experimenter displays the RED-grey card and to squeeze the ball with his left hand whenever the experimenter displays the GREEN-yellow card. After a few trials the child masters the task and performs it faultlessly. At this point, the experimenter changes the cards to see if the child has been responding to the dominant part of the stimulus—the colored circle—or the nondominant part—the background color. Thus, he may display a red circle on a yellow background and a green circle on grey. The results are clear-cut. The child responds to the dominant component—the colored circle.

Next, the experimenter attempts to change this natural dominance of the colored circle to its background with the aid of language. The experimenter explicitly points to the background colors and asks the child to press the ball with his right hand only at the appearance of a grey background and with his left hand only at the appearance of the yellow one. This attempt to reinforce the weaker component of the complex stimulus of circle-and-background has different effects depending on the age of the child. Children of age three and four, for the most part, do not readjust their behavior when given this verbal instruction. They continue to squeeze the ball entirely in terms of the stronger component, the colored circle. Children of ages four to five show an intermediate condition—they sometimes respond to background and sometimes to circle, but the effect is unstable. Only when the child is of age six and upwards can he, as a result of verbal instruction, begin to react consistently to the weaker component, the background.

The Russian experimenter pushes further. He asks whether it is possible to vary the age limits at which the action of speech will overcome the perceptual dominance of the stronger component in the complex stimulus. He finally succeeds by replacing the colored circles with red and green airplanes on the same grey and yellow backgrounds. The child is asked to press the ball with his right hand at the appearance of a red airplane on the *yellow* background (the experimenter adds that "the plane can fly when the sun is shining and the sky is yellow"); he is asked to press with his left hand at the appearance of a green airplane on the grey background (the experimenter adds that "when the weather is bad and when it rains the plane cannot fly—it must be stopped!"). With these instructions the backgrounds, which previously were the weaker components, now become dominant and the majority of children, even at age three, begin to react to the backgrounds and not to the figures.*

BUILT-IN AND NATURAL CONSTRAINTS

The various types of research methods we have just described—the naturalistic, the differential, and the experimental—can vary in terms of number and type of constraints imposed on the observer and the observational situation. Roughly, the naturalistic methods impose the fewest constraints and the experimental methods impose the most. In the naturalistic methods, the observer does not attempt to influence or interact with the behavior he is inter-

* A. R. Luria. *The role of speech in the regulation of normal and abnormal behavior.* Bethesda, Maryland: U. S. Dept. of Health, Education, and Welfare, Russian Scientific Translation Program, 1960.

Getting
the Facts

54

ested in. At one extreme, he may approach a situation with no prior restrictions on what he is going to observe or how he is going to record it. At this level are the kinds of observation of a community made by good journalists and anthropologists. Naturalistic observation by a psychologist is more likely to have somewhat more of a conceptual focus. The observer may still make every attempt to impose no restrictions on what can happen, but he may restrict his focus to certain aspects of behavior.

The clinical method as employed by Piaget typically imposes some constraints on the situation by initiating responses on the part of the subject. The experimenter confronts the child with a question or with a partially standardized task. His line of questioning obviously focuses on only certain kinds of information about the child's thought process. Although what happens once the task is presented is extremely variable and flexible, the investigator, by continually interacting with the child and by responding to the child's answers with more questions, interferes with and influences the results in ways that are hard to determine or assess.

The differential methods, especially in the form of interviews or questionnaires, place constraints on both observer and respondent. The observer is typically constrained to treat each individual in as identical a fashion as he can. To the extent that he does not observe each individual under "identical" circumstances, he is violating one of the fundamental principles of measurement—and measurement is one of the ideals of the differential approach. The respondent is constrained by being asked to respond to a standardized stimulus—a questionnaire, a standard set of oral questions, a test, or a standard task. Great variation exists in the degree of constraint. At one extreme—the open-ended questionnaire, for example—the subject is free to respond to the question in any manner and with any form of expression he chooses. At the other extreme, the subject may have to confine his responses to a given set of fixed categories—"Yes" or "No," "Same" or "Different," and so on. The differential methods may also vary in their constraints on the setting. Sometimes, as in surveys and public opinion polls, the respondent is interviewed on the street or in his home. At other times the respondents are assembled in groups or dealt with individually in classrooms or a standard testing room. In the psychophysical methods, which deal with how responses vary with changes in physical stimulation, the background and stimulus situation are almost completely constrained by the experimenter. To control background stimulation, a room may be soundproofed, made light-tight, and so forth. To control extraneous movements of the subject's head and eyes, he may be asked to place his head in a special headrest and fix his gaze upon a designated fixation point.

Field versus Laboratory Experiments

The experimental methods can vary in constraints almost as widely as can the differential methods. In a "field experiment," for example, the constraints and degree of control of the situation might be far less than is achieved with some of the differential methods, because a field experiment is conducted in a natural setting; the constraints on what can happen in the subject's environment, then, are minimal. What makes such an investigation an "experiment" is that the investigator introduces an independent variable into the situation. For example, S. Schachter and others conducted an experiment in a factory; the subjects were assembly-line workers who were performing their jobs under normal conditions.*

The experimenters, however, were able to expose one group of workers to an increase in typical everyday annoyances such as emphasis on housekeeping chores by the foreman, time-and-motion studies, and comments by the foreman on the quality of the work. An "equivalent" group of workers, on another shift, were carefully screened from such annoyances during the same two-week period that the first group was receiving the experimental treatment. At the end of this period, a minor change in the work routine was introduced into both groups. As expected, this minor change resulted in an increase in the number of defective units turned out by both assembly lines. But the group that had been screened from normal annoyances during the preceding two weeks quickly returned to a normal level of quality; the experimental group's rate of defects, on the other hand, persisted above normal over a longer period of time.

Such a field experiment has many of the features of naturalistic observation in that it is conducted under fairly normal conditions. But this very lack of constraint on what can happen in the situation makes such experiments far less conclusive and informative than those wherein the experimenter has more control over setting, subjects, and background factors. During the course of one of the replications of this industrial experiment, for example, a strike occurred. In another replication, a big snowstorm, unusual for that part of the country, resulted in many absentees, and substitute workers had to be employed on some of the assembly lines. Some of the attempts to create annoyances actually backfired. On one occasion, when the factory girls learned that motion pictures were going to be taken as part of a time-and-motion study, instead of responding with the expected complaints, they came to work the next day with make-up and dresses rather than their normal attire of overalls. On the other hand, some attempts to make the comparison group feel more secure actually created the opposite effect.

The problems illustrated by the field experiment raise the issue of the "artificiality" of laboratory experiments. The advantage of observations made under naturalistic methods and in field experiments is that they are obviously relevant to real-life behavior. Yet, this illusion of relevance or actual relevance may be obtained at the cost of vagueness, ambiguity, and imprecision. The results of such observations may be suggestive, but they rarely are conclusive because too many factors must be left uncontrolled.

One way out of this box is to parallel, whenever possible, field experiments

* S. Schachter, B. Willerman, L. Festinger, and R. Hyman. Emotional disruption and industrial productivity. *J. appl. Psychol.*, 1961, 201–213.

with laboratory experiments. In the field experiment that was described, attempts at reproducing the major results with laboratory experiments are actually taking place. In the laboratory, the experimenter can constrain the setting and the extraneous background events. He can schedule annoyances and distractions as precisely as he pleases and he can present identical conditions and stimulation to different groups. He further has greater leeway in the assignment of individuals to different treatments, thereby eliminating or taking into account initial differences between groups. He can control other differences such as the time of day, the physical setting, the foreman. He can choose a task that is more sensitive to external stress and one that can yield observations that are quantifiable. He can further constrain his subjects by means of instructions, placement, or physical means. In this way, he can pin down more precisely what factors are operating in the situation and how much of the observed effect is due to each.

Rigor versus Relevance

Thus we see that the degree of constraint in the laboratory experiment allows the experimenter to answer precisely certain kinds of questions. At the very same time, however, this control is obtained by creating a highly artificial situation. The subjects know that they are participating in an experiment. They have usually volunteered to participate to gain classroom credit or to earn some cash. The situation and task bear little resemblance to the reality of a factory with its social cliques, its overtones of management-labor strife, its seasonal fluctuations and layoffs, its humming machinery, its coffee breaks and lunch hours, its turnover, jealousies, and the like.

The answer to this apparent dilemma between observations that have relevance only for a given problem and observations that are rigorous and reliable is that neither laboratory experiments nor naturalistic or field studies can stand alone as devices for furthering scientific inquiry. A psychological inquiry gains its relevance and significance, in large part, because of the experimenter's naturalistic and casual observations before he introduces constraints into his gathering of data on which his conclusions will depend. The inquiry gains its reliability and rigor, on the other hand, because of the constraints and controls that the experimenter can exercise on the setting and the other variables that will be used to test the validity of his initial ideas and hypotheses.

In a well-conducted inquiry, then, there need be no conflict between the ideals of relevance and of rigor—each can be achieved by different kinds of activities at different stages of the inquiry. What apparently concerns many critics of studies in psychology is the confusion that sometimes exists between constraints due to method and constraints that reflect actual relationships in nature. Such confusion seems especially likely when investigators uncritically adopt a method that has been successful in one domain of inquiry and routinely apply it in another domain.

Knowing What To Ignore

A psychologist always has to keep in mind that a previously productive method has succeeded as much by what it does not allow to happen as by what it does allow to happen. Pavlov's success with the conditioned reflex depended on a number of constraints which he introduced in the observational procedure. He quickly discovered that the conditioned reflex was a very unstable and difficult phenomenon to produce in a lawful manner because of a variety of extraneous influences—noises, the presence of strangers, other dogs, the animal's prior handling, the dog's orientation at the time the stimulus was presented, the behavior of the experimenter—all could influence the outcome. His first task was to find the conditions under which he could reliably and objectively observe this phenomenon. For this purpose he gradually imposed constraints on the environment—a soundproofed room, special devices for automatically delivering food and signals, and the removal of the experimenter. He also introduced standardization into the preparation and handling of the animal prior to the experiment. He also placed constraints on what the animal could do and on his orientation by training him to wait patiently upon a platform and by further restraining him with a harness.

Pavlov further simplified his task by observing only the reaction of the salivary gland. Other glands were more complex in their activity; and though he realized that the animal also responded with motor activity—turning his head, opening his mouth, chewing, and the like—Pavlov deliberately avoided using observations of motor activity as data. By means of these constraints on what was observed, what could happen, and what the animal could do, Pavlov achieved his goal of discovering lawful relationships between artificially established signals and salivary secretions. These constraints, in terms of Pavlov's conceptual focus and problem—studying the connection between stimulation and nervous regulation of glands—were quite appropriate and ingenious. Their success is attested to by the fame of their creator.

The success of Pavlov's procedure, it cannot be too strongly emphasized, depended on his deliberately controlling the situation to exclude many possible sources of variation that might mask the relationship he was after. Pavlov's procedure was successful because it enabled him to select from nature just those pieces of information that were relevant to the questions he was asking. His success lay as much in what he was able to omit from the situation by placing constraints on it as it was in what nature, in also placing constraints, put into the situation.

But the very reason for the success of Pavlov's observational procedure can result, when his methods and data are employed in the service of other conceptual focuses, in faulty conclusions. Because of the constraints in the conditioning experiment, the Pavlovian model works best with what we today refer to as "sign" learning. Only one type of response was observed—the amount of salivary flow. In Pavlov's classic experiment, then, the only change that could occur was in the nature of the stimuli that could affect this response. The experiment was so arranged that it focused on substituting a conditioned stimulus, say a bell, for an unconditioned stimulus, say the sight of food. What the animal learned was to salivate to the bell where before he salivated only to the food. This kind of learning, where the same response is applied to a new stimulus, is the only kind of learning that can occur in the Pavlovian experiment.

Until recently many futile arguments and confusions arose because psychologists failed to distinguish between the constraints that are built into the observations by the conditioning experiment and the constraints that result from the way the organism is constituted. Thus, arguments and debates raged about whether all learning was, as exhibited in the Pavlovian experiment, a matter of substituting one stimulus for another one.

In Pavlov's experiment, the evidence for learning consists of salivating to a new stimulus. The old response and the new response, then, are of the same kind. Now look at the experimental arrangement of Edward L. Thorndike's puzzle box experiments at the turn of the century. A cat was confined to a cage-like box. Food was placed outside the box just beyond the reach of the cat. The cat's first responses were to try to squeeze out of the box through the slats. But it did not succeed. The cat then engaged in a lot of other activity. Eventually, by accident, it stepped on the lever that released the lock to the box. After several repetitions of this experience, the cat eventually learned to make immediately the appropriate movement to release it from confinement. Such learning is what we now call "instrumental" or "solution" learning. In somewhat simple terms, we can say that the animal learns to employ a *new response* to the *same stimulus*. By the very way the experiment is set up, the only way the animal can demonstrate learning in Thorndike's experiment is to learn a new response.

More recently, psychologists have devised experimental situations where an animal has to employ both sign learning and solution learning. In one kind of experiment the animal first learns that a buzzer is a sign for a forthcoming electric shock (conditioning); next he learns how to avoid this forthcoming shock by jumping over a barrier (solution learning).

We could recite many more illustrations to make this very important point. Controlled procedures of observation succeed in giving precise answers to certain kinds of questions by excluding certain possibilities. Each procedure that has been devised to produce scientific data does so by building certain constraints into what can take place and what can be observed. Consequently, the more precisely a technique can answer one kind of question, the more likely it will be that this same technique will give the wrong answer or actually obscure the answer to another type of question.

Processing the Data

"We must first accurately define the conditions of each phenomenon; this is true biological accuracy, and, without this preliminary study, all numerical data are inaccurate, and the more inaccurate because they include figures which mislead and impose on us by a false appearance of accuracy." (Claude Bernard, 1865.)

Once the data have been collected they have to be reduced to a form in which they can be readily interpreted within the investigator's conceptual system. The analysis of data can be compared with the process of digestion. When food, which corresponds to the data in this analogy

5

is ingested by an organism, it cannot be used by the body until it is broken down and reconstituted into a form that can be assimilated. Various foodstuffs require different degrees of time and different combinations of alimentary activity for this process. The digestive process has to accommodate itself in a highly specific manner to each type of food. Likewise, an investigator has to accommodate his procedures for analyzing data to fit the nature of the original observations. Some data-gathering procedures, such as readings in resistance units from the dial of a psychogalvanometer, provide initial data in the form of numbers. In such cases the investigator can begin his processing by applying statistical methods directly to these numbers. On the other hand, open-ended interviews provide initial data that need additional processing and coding before the psychologist is ready to begin statistical summarization. Different sorts of data, then, demand different kinds of handling before they are reduced to a form in which the investigator can interpret his results.

WEAK AND STRONG METHODS

We have seen how the manner of collecting data can impose constraints on the forms the data can take. We shall now also discover that various procedures for summarizing, describing, and generalizing from data also impose constraints on the forms of the results. In the early stages of an inquiry, it is just as important to avoid imposing a premature form of data analysis as it is to avoid imposing too many constraints on the observational procedure. When we are trying to get a feel for the kinds of units, variables, and relationships that may be significant in a new area, the so-called "weak" methods of data-analysis may be appropriate. These weak methods involve few assumptions about what form is most natural for describing a new topic. Indeed, their orientation is toward finding the kind of descriptive model that best conforms to the subject matter in an area of inquiry.

As we move to later stages of an inquiry, where our questions become sharper and more specific, then "strong" methods of analyzing the data become appropriate. These stronger methods, by making many more assumptions about the measurement model to which the data must conform, place many constraints on the possible relationships that can result. Rather than contribute to the discovery of what the shape of the data are, they impose a shape on the data, enabling the researcher to answer rather specific questions. These strong methods, when appropriate, lend rigor and "power" to the results and enable the investigator to state his conclusions in fairly precise terms. And, just as was the case in the collection of data, these more constrained analyses gain both their power to answer specific questions and their extreme inflexibility to deal with alternative questions by ruthlessly suppressing several alternative possibilities.

Perhaps a concrete example can serve to introduce some of the issues that we shall touch upon in this chapter. In a famous experiment, the social psychologist Solomon Asch investigated the effects of group pressures on an individual's behavior under conditions where the group unanimously contradicted the evidence of his senses.* In this experiment a group of eight subjects was given the task of matching the length of a given line, the standard line, with one of three unequal lines, the comparison lines. Prior to the experiment seven of these subjects, without the knowledge of the eighth person, had been given instructions to respond deliberately and *unanimously* with the *wrong* line at certain points in the experiment. As far as the eighth, or critical, subject was concerned, the experiment involved making perceptual judgments of lines under conditions where discrimination was fairly easy and clear-cut. On the first trial the experimenter would display a standard line of 10 inches, and ask the subjects to announce out loud, one by one, which of the three comparison lines was of equal length to the standard, the comparison lines being of lengths 8¾, 10, and 8 inches respectively. Each subject, in turn, announced that the second line was the correct one. Another easy comparison involving a 2-inch line was presented on the second trial and all eight subjects had no difficulty in calling out the correct match. But suddenly something was amiss. The experimenter held up a 3-inch line as the standard. One by one, each of the first seven subjects chose a comparison line that was 3¾ inches long rather than the line that was 3 inches long. All told, in a series of 18 trials, there were 12 occasions in which the critical subject was confronted with what must have been an obvious contradiction between his perceptual experience and the unanimous judgment of the other members of the group. As Asch describes this individual's plight:

> The outstanding person—the critical subject—whom we had placed in the position of a *minority of one* in the midst of a *unanimous majority*—was the object of investigation. He faced, possibly for the first time in his life, a situation in which a group unanimously contradicted the evidence of his senses.

Asch collected two kinds of information from each critical subject. The major data were in the form of the number of critical trials on which the subject went along with the majority when the majority opinion was obviously wrong. Out of 50 subjects, for example, not one individual yielded to majority opinion on all 12 critical trials, but one subject yielded on 11 of the trials and as many as 14 subjects yielded on more than half of the critical trials. Only

* S. E. Asch. Effects of group pressure upon the modification and distortion of judgments. In Eleanor E. Maccoby, T. M. Newcomb, E. L. Hartley (eds.). *Readings in social psychology*. New York: Holt, Rinehart and Winston, 1958, pp. 174–183.

13 out of the 50 subjects failed to yield on at least one of the trials. The other kind of information came from an intensive interview with each subject after the experiment. During this interview the experimenter carefully explained the true purpose of the experiment to the subject and reassured him concerning the normality of his performance.

The interviews provided qualitative information to help explain the subjects' reactions and behavior on the critical trials. The interviews, for example, suggested that among the subjects who failed to be influenced by the group, there were major differences in their reasons. Some subjects showed an independence that was clearly based on *confidence* in their own perceptual ability. Other subjects seemed to be responding to conform to what they thought were the experimenter's desires. And some remained independent purely for the sake of being different. Among those who yielded to group pressure were a few who seemed genuinely unaware that there was anything wrong in the situation. As far as the experimenter could tell, the perception of these individuals was actually distorted to agree with the group majority. Most of the yielders, however, were quite aware that their judgments were not in line with their perceptions; but they went along with the majority because they lacked confidence in their own perceptual accuracy and felt that the majority was probably correct. Still another set of subjects believed that their own perceptions were correct, but went along with the majority because they did not want to appear different from the others.

Although our interest in this experiment, at this point, is to illustrate how the investigator processes his primary data, I spent some time describing the secondary data, or qualitative information Asch obtained, because it illustrates how the use of both quantitative and qualitative data can increase an experimenter's grasp of what is going on. Qualitative data, moreover, supply the researcher with several leads and guides for the design of further experiments. Many investigators deprive themselves of this opportunity to add a qualitative background to their experiments by failing to participate personally in the actual collection of the data. Such researchers sometimes oversimplify the outcomes of their experiments; they might, for example, lump all yielders together and all nonyielders together and try to find one explanation to account for all the individuals within these two divisions. Without having pursued the matter with supplementary information, they would be unable to do otherwise. But by probing somewhat beneath the bare classification given to him by his index of yielding, Asch come up with the incidental observation—one which of course, forms the basis not for a conclusion but for a conjecture that might be tested in a later experiment—that two individuals might yield for two quite different psychological reasons.

Like all good experiments, Asch's study includes a control group, 37 subjects who were run under the same identical set of judgments as were the 50 critical subjects but made their judgments without the pressure of knowing what other members were doing. Table 1 shows the number of subjects who fell into each of the four subcategories formed by the dichotomies into which we can classify each subject—control or experimental group, and "no errors" or "at least one error" (in the direction of the majority estimates).

TABLE 1

Results of Perceptual Judgment Task

| | Independent Variable | |
Dependent Variable	Control Group	Experimental Group
No errors	35	13
One or more errors	2	37

This table shows that in the control group only two individuals, or 5.4 per cent of the 37 subjects, made any errors on the judgment task. This suggests that, when no group pressure is applied to an individual, almost everyone can select the right line in the experimental situation easily and correctly. Of the two individuals who did make errors, one made only one mistake and the other made two mistakes. The importance of this baseline becomes clear when we look at the performance of the subjects who were subjected to contradictory pressures by the group on 12 of their judgments. Here we see that 37 out of the 50 subjects in this category, or 74 per cent, yielded to group pressure in making one or more errors in judgment in the direction of the group consensus. If we did not have the results from the control group, the results from the experimental group would be ambiguous. We would not know whether such errors would occur in the absence of the group pressures.

FROM RECORDS TO DATA

We want to use the outcome of this experiment to illustrate some features that come under the heading of processing the data. In the first place there is the idea of *classification*. On each of the 12 critical trials the experimenter observes what the subject does when his turn appears. If the subject is in the experimental group he announces his choice among the three comparison lines publicly. He may indicate his choice in a variety of ways—he may report "the middle line," or "the second from the left," or "the second longest line," or he may point to his choice. Furthermore, he may shout his answer, he may whisper it, he may hestiate, he may qualify it with some phrases such as "I think . . .," or "I may be cuckoo, but. . . ." He may even refrain from making a choice or do so only at the urging of the investigator. Although the experimenter may note some of these qualitative aspects of the subject's response, the basic "fact" that he records for this subject and this trial is a record of his choice. From this record, on each trial and for each subject, the experimenter will begin further processing of the outcomes until he can reduce the mass of recorded observations into a form that can readily be interpreted in terms of his conceptual framework.

Notice that the initial record of what takes place, sometimes called the *protocol* or the *raw data,* is already an abstraction from a much more complex event. Many things that possibly could have been recorded are omitted. Features of the subject's expression, extraneous noises that may be barely audible outside the experimental room, certain gestures and qualities of the subject's voice, the time he takes to report his choice, and many, many other things cannot possibly be recorded. Even an attempt to capture as much of the situation as possible with the initial record still does not avoid the necessity of abstracting only some of the features that take place within the total situation. In some studies of what takes place in psychotherapy, for example, investigators, fearing that they may inadvertently overlook important clues in the situation, have made their original records in the form of colored motion pictures accompanied by a stereophonic sound recording. Even with such a rich record, the investigators have had to do without many additional aspects of the situation, such as odorous, tactual, and other cues that escaped their recording devices. Furthermore, many physiological and microscopic events are omitted from this initial record. More importantly, starting with a protocol that is a reasonably faithful replica of an original situation does not avoid the necessity of abstracting and omitting many details if one is to summarize and find order in the observations. Rather, it postpones the summarization to a later step in the investigation (as many investigators have found to their sorrow).

It is important to grasp that the so-called "objective events" every investigator starts with are already abstractions from reality. What we have just said about the necessity of abstracting observations from more complex events in the Asch situation is true of every scientific investigation. In psychology it is all too easy to treat what an investigator calls "the stimulus" and "the response" as "the hard facts." But both the "stimulus" and the "response," as used in psychological research, are instances of general classes; they never stand for particular concrete occurrences.

In Asch's experiment, the first step is to transform the record of each subject's choices into the basic classification of whether his choice represents an "error" or a correct choice (a selection that corresponds with the actual physical match). This transformation is accomplished by ignoring qualitative differences among subjects and the manner in which they make their choice. A further reduction of information is accomplished by treating each of the critical trials as equivalent. The dependent variable for each subject will be a number that can vary from 0 to 12 depending on how many of his trials were classified as "errors." In assigning each subject to a category on the basis of the number of errors he has made, differences between trials are ignored. Two subjects will be classified as having made the same number of errors, and therefore as being "equivalent" on the dependent variable, if each has made three errors even if one subject made all his errors on the first three trials and the other subject made his three errors on the last three trials. For some purposes and questions it may be important to differentiate among subjects on the order and pattern in which they make their errors; for other purposes, especially where a limited number of subjects can be used, it may be necessary to ignore differences that are related to the particular trials.

THE NECESSITY FOR DATA-REDUCTION

This latter point is worth further comment. Suppose that Asch did not want to lump together subjects on his dependent variable unless they had made their errors on identical trials. In order to classify all subjects who make three errors out of 12 trials as equivalent only if their errors are on the same trials, Asch would have to distinguish 220 different categories just for this number of errors. Indeed, if Asch wanted to allow for each possible distinguishable pattern of errors on the 12 trials, he would have to allow for 4,096 classifications. In an experiment employing only 87 subjects, an attempt to make such fine distinctions, however desirable, would be futile.

No matter how many categories the investigator wishes to employ, at some point he has to summarize and describe his results by pooling categories together in some way or other. He has to do so for two important reasons. First, unless he reduces the patterns of responses to a small number of summary classes or finds simple relationships among his variables, he cannot interpret or understand his findings in terms of a conceptual system. Second, he cannot communicate these findings without first reducing them to summary form. Try to imagine making sense out of a presentation of the data from Asch's experiment that merely reported the actual pattern of choices made by each subject. At the very least, you would find yourself rearranging the data, seeking for order and similarities, and looking for ways to reduce the complexity by assembling patterns together.

As it turns out, we can answer some interesting and important questions about the outcome of Asch's experiment by making an even greater reduction of the data. Since almost no one in the control group makes a mistake in the judgment task (out of 444 control trials, only 3 errors were made), it seems sensible, as a first simplification, to split the 87 subjects into two categories on the dependent variable: those subjects who never make a mistake and those who make at least one mistake. Such a simplification is achieved at the expense of treating as equivalent a subject who makes only one error and a subject who makes as many as 11 errors. On the other hand, the simplification has the advantage of not only making the outcome easier to describe, but also of making the number of individuals within each classification reasonably large. For certain purposes, such as making appropriate statistical estimates or inferences, it is necessary to have classes with reasonably large numbers of members.

When we come back to the issue of averaging and pooling observations, the important point to recall is not that lumping individuals and observations into equivalent categories is either "good" or "bad." Any procedure for processing scientific data—indeed, any scientific observation—begins and ends with the omission of many details and differences. When we report averages, numbers of people in categories, correlation coefficients, or summaries of our data, we do so only by violating a variety of distinctions that, for many purposes, may turn out to be quite important. What is important, is that, depending on the question we are asking, some forms of pooling and reduction make more sense than do others. All forms of reduction make several assumptions about what kinds of things can be treated as equivalent, what kinds of differences can be ignored, and what kinds of combinations make sense in terms of how the "real world" is put together.

Furthermore, some forms of data-reduction make more assumptions than do others. In each case, the relevance or irrelevance of certain pooling and summarizing procedures must be judged in terms of the investigator's conceptual system and the kinds of questions he wants to put to his data. Where investigators seem to employ grossly inappropriate procedures or confuse restrictions they have imposed on the data with relationships that exist in nature, this should not be taken as an argument against the employment of statistics and pooling procedures; rather, it should be taken as a warning that we must be careful to match our processing methods to our conceptual framework. The various constraints that we impose on our observations and our data are neither harmful nor harmless in themselves. They lead to distortion and faulty research only when they are applied automatically and without a full comprehension of the limitations being imposed by the method of inquiry rather than by the forces of nature.

RELATIONSHIPS BETWEEN VARIABLES

Once an investigator has coded his data into the basic categories of his independent and dependent variables, he can begin to derive some kind of *description* of his results on the basis of the *distribution* of individuals among these categories. In the Asch experiment, where we have reduced each variable into a dichotomy, the idea of distribution is easy to grasp. We can describe the outcome of this experiment, as exhibited in the preceding table, in terms of the frequencies of occurrence of individuals within each of four data classifications. In an investigation of this sort, what the investigator chiefly is interested in is the relationship of the dependent variable to each level of the independent variable. In the Asch experiment, the distribution of subjects in the experimental condition, for example, is 13 and 37; in the control condition the distribution is 35 and 2. Because the total number of subjects differs for each value of the independent variable (50 and 37), the comparison of these two distributions is made easier if we convert the actual frequencies for each distribution into relative frequencies, or percentages. When this is done, we get the comparison as shown in Table 2.

TABLE 2

Results (in percentages) of the Perceptual Judgment Task

Errors	Control Group	Experimental Group
None	94.5	26.0
At least one	5.4	74.0

In this experiment the outcome is sufficiently striking that not much further comparison is needed to summarize the results. But, typically, the results are rarely this clear-cut, or the data are distributed over a larger set of categories. Under such circumstances it frequently helps both the investigator and his readers to have a pictorial or graphical representation of the distributions. Most of the time, a well-chosen graph can quickly and immediately display differences in the distributions that may not be readily apparent from the numbers listed in a complicated table. One possible graphic representation of the two distributions in this experiment, for example, is shown in Figure 1.

Figure 2 displays another manner of comparing the two distributions. In this graph, to display more completely the differences between the two conditions, we have broken the dependent variable down into its original 12 subdivisions in terms of number of errors; furthermore, we have super-

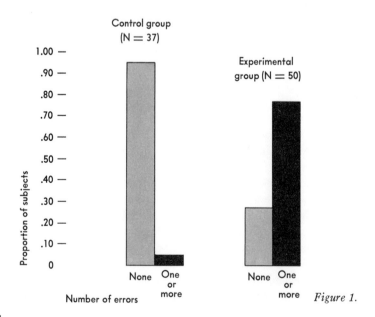

Figure 1.

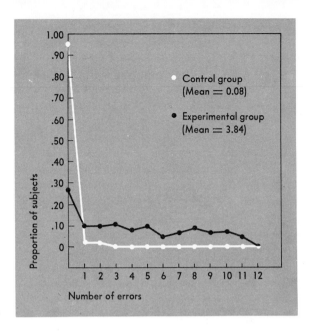

Figure 2.

imposed the lines connecting both distributions so that the reader can more readily study the differences between the distribution of errors in the two groups.

This second graph displays quite clearly some features about the distributions that would be not so evident from a table and that would be completely missing from a simple statistical summarization. The means, or averages, of the two distributions are indicated on the graphs. The average number of errors per subject in the control group is 0.08, while the average number of errors for the subjects in the critical group is 3.84. This comparison of the averages conveys some useful information about the outcome of this experiment. In many other experiments, where the shapes of the different distributions that are being compared are more similar than the two distributions here, the differences between the averages actually summarize most of the useful information in the experiment. In the present illustration, however, the mere statement that the average is 3.84 per subject in the critical group hardly does justice to the nature of the distribution. In fact, as the graph displays, the most interesting feature of this distribution is its great spread, or variability. In this condition we find subjects categorized at every possible value except 12 errors. Furthermore, with the exception of the 13 subjects who made no errors, there is no particular place in the distribution that is especially typical. The most characteristic aspect of this experimental condition, then, seems to be that it disperses subjects over the entire range of possibilities, from a large number to a small number of errors. The graph, in this case, seems to be the easiest and most appropriate manner of depicting this outcome. Depending on one's theory and depending on the actual distributions obtained, different modes of summarizing and presenting data may be appropriate. By the same token, many ways of summarizing and presenting results can obscure or even distort the actual relationships between an independent variable and a dependent variable.

Both the tabular and graphic summaries are ways of describing the distributions actually observed in an experiment. An investigator is not interested in the observed differences between these distributions as such. He knows that many factors may be affecting the results. For one thing, the 50 individuals in the experimental group are not the same individuals who compose the control group. Although we assume that the experimenter took pains to minimize or randomize initial differences between these two groups, we know that it is not possible to guarantee that the subjects in both groups are actually equivalent in every important respect in terms of the experimental task. All we can hope for is that *on the average* as many individuals who might tend to make mistakes on the judgment task in the absence of group consensus were assigned to both groups. Yet, it is possible that some of the individuals in the experimental group would have made errors even if they had been in the control group. Furthermore, as we can tell from looking at the distribution of results, in the experimental group not every individual will respond in the same way to group pressure. It is conceivable that more individuals who would resist such pressure found their way by accident into the control group than into the experimental group.

In general, we can think of two sources of error that might produce observed differences in the distributions which are *not* due to the experimental variable. One source of errors produces a bias that consistently favors one group or the other; we call this *constant error*. A constant error could occur in the present experiment, for example, if each condition were carried out at different times. If, for example, the experimenter first conducted all his sessions with the experimental condition before he conducted the sessions with the control condition, the difference in time might indirectly produce differences in results. Word might leak out to future subjects about the nature of the experiment. Being on guard, they might take pains to be accurate in their judgments. This factor could then possibly make the control subjects look more accurate than the experimental ones, but the reason would be other than differences in treatments. Or the subjects who are gathered for later sessions might be from a different pool, and hence differ from those who were available for the experimental conditions. Or the control sessions may be handled by different experimenters or otherwise be conducted in a way that differentially affects the responses of the subjects. In the present experiment, for example, subjects in the control condition wrote their responses, whereas subjects in the experimental condition vocalized theirs. To the extent that this response mode can produce a difference in the judgments made, it would produce a constant error by differentially affecting the outcome of the experiment in a way that might be falsely attributed to the independent variable. Other constant errors, as has been shown by R. Rosenthal and others can slip into the results through unconscious cues the experimenter transmits to his subjects.*

There are no simple answers for dealing with constant errors. The experimenter, through experience and training, learns how to anticipate many of the most serious sources of such errors. He attempts to assign subjects to conditions, to counterbalance treatments, to build in various safeguards that minimize these possible inaccuracies. A large part of the progress of scientific inquiry in any particular domain, including several areas of psychology, depends on uncovering such constant errors and demonstrating that they could have been the cause of results in previous experiments. In recent experiments on the perception of emotionally charged words (obscene phrases, for example), the results clearly indicated that subjects had more difficulty in recognizing emotional words than in recognizing neutral words under the same viewing conditions. At first these differences were attributed to the effects of emotional meanings on perceptual recognition. Later work, however, revealed that at least some of these differences in the data were the result of constant errors due to the differences in the infrequency of emotional words as compared with the neutral words. When the emotional words are equated with the neutral words for frequency of occurrence in everyday reading, then much of the original difference disappears.

The other class of errors can be called *variable errors* in that their effects are likely to operate equally on the results in all the experimental conditions. An experimenter assumes that such errors, in the long run, will tend to cancel one another out. For example, even with the extremely simple perceptual task Asch employed, two subjects in the control group still managed to make at least one incorrect judgment. Presumably, if the subjects are assigned randomly to the two conditions, such errors of judgment will be distributed evenly over both experimental conditions. To the extent that this is so they will cancel each other out. Variable errors are often called *sampling errors* because they tend to produce variation in the results that are due in part to the sample of subjects assigned to each condition. If the experiment is repeated, the particular sample of subjects assigned to each condition will, of course, differ with each repetition. By accidents of sampling, for example, the actual percentage of subjects who make errors in the control group may be higher than the observed 5 per cent or it could be much lower. And in another experiment, Dame Fortune might arrange to have more subjects in the experimental group who fail to yield than the 26 per cent that happened to be in the particular sample employed in Asch's first experiment. Or, being

* R. Rosenthal. On the social psychology of the psychological experiment. *Amer. Sci.*, 1963, 51, 268–283.

the unpredictable prankster she is, Dame Fortune may arrange to have many more subjects at the other end of the scale. At any rate, if we repeated this experiment, we certainly would not expect to find again exactly 74 per cent of the critical subjects and 5.4 per cent of the control subjects making at least one error. At best, we would hope to find that the difference between the two distributions is of the same form, and roughly of the same magnitude, as we observed in the present case.

Other sources of variable errors lie in the many uncontrollable features of the real world, such as the particular mood and expectations of individual subjects, variability in an experimenter's mannerisms when he faces the different groups, errors in recording and analyzing the data, and mistakes made by the subjects in reporting or writing down their observations. The object or ideal of many features of experimental control, indeed, is to minimize as many of these sources of variable error as possible in order for us to see more clearly the relationships of interest.

MAKING INFERENCES FROM THE DATA

One way an investigator attempts to cope with the existence of variable and sampling errors is by means of *statistical inference*. The phrase statistical inference refers to a set of procedures for estimating the extent to which observed differences are due to *chance,* or variable errors. In reporting the differences between two or more observed distributions, an investigator is obliged to do more than merely describe the actual distributions or summarize the observed difference. He is expected to accompany each outcome with an estimate of the probability that the observed difference was due to variable factors. Unless this probability is reasonably low, he is discouraged from attributing the outcome to the effect of his experimental variable. In other words, the investigator does more than summarize the outcome of his experiment by characterizing the distributions of results. He attempts to go beyond this description by demonstrating that the observed differences or relationships are not plausibly explained in terms of chance factors.

Again we can employ the results of Asch's experiment to illustrate this point. In any investigation, a psychologist's immediate goal is to discover (or test) a relationship between the variables of interest. The processing of the data is a series of operations that transform the initial observations into variables. Once the observations have been reduced to variables, the next step is to examine the relationships among these variables. In the Asch experiment, the experimenter *observed* the subject's responses on the critical trials, *recorded* the subject's choice of a comparison line, transformed this record into the categories "correct" or incorrect," and, finally, transformed these primary *data* into a *variable* by adding up the number of "incorrect" choices for each subject. For the purposes of the present analysis we have further transformed the experimenter's dependent variable from one that could assume

13 possible values (0 through 12) to one that can assume two values, "no errors" and "at least one." The question for the investigator, at this point, is whether there is a relationship between the values on this dependent variable and the experimental treatment.

We can demonstrate a *relationship* between two variables if we can show that the values assumed with one variable depend on the values of the second variable. If a subject's classification into control or experimental condition does not affect his subsequent classification on the dependent variable, then we say that the two variables are *independent* and that no relationship exists between them. There would be no relationship between our two variables, for example, if the proportion of individuals who make at least one error is the same under both experimental conditions. However, as we have already pointed out, even if no relationship really exists between group pressure and number of errors, we would expect to observe a difference between the two proportions in our results. The question the investigator tries to answer by statistical means is whether the observed relationship is "statistically significant." Is the actual difference between 74 per cent and 5.4 per cent in this experiment sufficiently large to enable us to reject chance as the sole cause?

To test for the possibility that the observed relationship is due to chance, the investigator performs an operation that we might label the *significance test ritual*. The term "ritual" appropriately describes this operation because most investigators perform such a test as a matter of routine and typically carry out each step of the operation automatically or by following the rules as laid out in a standard textbook. The ritual more or less involves the following routine:

1. First the investigator sets up what is called "the null hypothesis"; roughly this hypothesis states that the observed relationship is a matter of chance. More formally, it says that if we repeated the experiment an indefinitely large number of times, the distribution of differences between the two proportions would tend to the average of zero. In other words, the experimenter makes certain assumptions about how the results of a large number of experiments would be distributed if the true difference was zero. He then calculates, on the assumption that his experimental outcome is a random selection from a larger population of possible results, what the probability would be of getting the particular difference he observes; if this probability is lower than a conventional level, then he concludes that the results were not due to chance. If this probability is not lower than this conventional level, then he cannot conclude, according to convention, that the results were not due to chance.

2. Next the investigator chooses a "level of significance." If the probability of obtaining his present result is less than this level, then he rejects chance as an alternative. For most purposes, the conventional level of significance is typically .05, or 5 out of 100. Sometimes, for more stringent tests, the level chosen is .01.

3. The investigator also decides on what type or form of "statistic" he is going to calculate from his data. To some extent, the nature of his data—such as frequency or measurement variables—decides the form of statistic that he will use. In addition, the investigator has a choice of alternative tests to employ depending on what kinds of assumptions he is willing to make beforehand about the nature of his distributions. Whatever the case, the tests are designed on the basis that the investigator selects his statistic before he looks at his data. Otherwise he might be tempted to try a variety of tests until he finds one that gives him the results he desires. And, to the extent that the investigator indulges in such attempts to find ways to make his data "significant," he negates the rationale for making statistical tests and will tend to report, as real, relationships that have no basis in fact.

In the present situation, where two proportions or distributions are to be compared, the investigator will probably employ the chi-square statistic. This statistic provides a number that will be close to 1.00 if the differences between the two percentages are what one would expect on the basis of chance and will get progressively larger as the difference between the two observed distributions gets larger.

4. The investigator sets up a "critical region" by designating which values of the statistic will lead him to reject the hypothesis of chance. In the present comparison, if the chi-square turns out to be larger than 3.84 (a value which can be obtained from standard tables), then it falls in the "critical region"; a value of chi-square of this magnitude or larger, will occur less than 5 per cent of the time if the true difference between the two proportions is zero. For the relationship in the Asch data, the difference between the proportions of 74 and 5.4 per cent results in a chi-square of approximately 38. Because this value is larger than the critical one of 3.84, the investigator would reject the "null hypothesis" at the 5 per cent level of significance and conclude that there is a significant difference between the two distributions. As a matter of fact, the probability of obtaining a chi-square this large on the basis of chance alone is considerably less than one in a thousand.

Having reached this stage in the analysis, the investigator has completed one phase of his inquiry. He has demonstrated, according to accepted convention, that he has obtained a relationship that cannot be attributed to chance factors. When he now goes beyond this step to speculate on the nature of this relationship and to interpret it in terms of his conceptual system, we enter into that phase we have labeled "interpretation of the data," a subject that is the topic of the next chapter. In the remainder of this chapter we shall elaborate somewhat on some of the issues raised by the steps we have illustrated in the processing of the data from Asch's experiment. Other kinds of data and investigations raise issues that differ from some of the particulars that we see in Asch's data. But the general approach of going from observation to data, from data to variable, from variable to relationship, and from observed relationship to inference about relationship in the larger population, typifies the steps in processing of data from psychological investigations.

Within recent years psychologists have gradually become disenchanted with the ability of statistical methods automatically to further their research. Currently, many of the elder statesmen in the field of psychological research are calling for an "agonizing reappraisal" of the proper role of statistics in psychological inquiry. In part, this disillusionment grows out of recent controversies among psychologists about the role of group averages as opposed to the study of single individuals. A second factor is the ever-increasing number of studies in which the uncritical use of statistical procedures seems to obscure and hinder discovery rather than clarify and aid it. A third factor seems to be the tendency of many investigators to select their problems to fit existing statistical methods rather than the other way around. In fact, some psychologists seem to identify themselves with a particular statistical tool—factor analysis, for example—rather than a substantive issue or problem. And, finally, there is controversy among the statisticians themselves about questions that cut to the very foundations of the assumptions on which statistical usage is based. For those psychologists who have found the need to master statistical reasoning the most painful and unsuccessful phase of their educational preparation, the heated debates among statisticians over what statistics is and is not must come as welcome reassurance. They are not the only ones who are confused by statistics.

The abuse of averages has long been recognized as a hindrance to good research. In 1865 Claude Bernard was already complaining about the faulty use of averages in research. His complaints at that time have the same foundation, and are just as timely, as are the current complaints about the use of statistical summaries by Professor B. F. Skinner and his followers. Bernard's argument is worth quoting at length: *

Another very frequent application of mathematics to biology is the use of averages which, in medicine and physiology, leads, so to speak, necessarily to error. There are doubtless several reasons for this; but the greatest obstacle to applying calculations to physiological phenomena is still, at bottom, the excessive complexity which prevents their being definite and comparable one with another. By destroying the biological character of phenomena, the use of *averages* in physiology and medicine usually gives only apparent accuracy to the results. From our point of view, we may distinguish between several kinds of averages; physical averages, chemical averages and physiological and pathological averages. If, for instance, we observe the number of pulsations and the degree of blood pressure by means of the oscillations of a manometer throughout one day, and if we take the average of all our figures to get the true or average blood pressure and to learn the true average number of pulsations, we shall simply have wrong numbers. In fact, the pulse decreases in number and intensity when we are fasting and increases during digestion or under different influences of movement and rest; all the biological characteristics of the phenomenon disappear in the average.

* C. Bernard. *An introduction to the study of experimental medicine.* New York: Dover, 1957, pp. 134–135.

Chemical averages are also often used. If we collect a man's urine during twenty-four hours and mix all this urine to analyze the average, we get an analysis of a urine which simply does not exist; for urine, when fasting, is different from urine during digestion. A startling instance of this kind was invented by a physiologist who took urine from a railroad station urinal where people of all nations passed, and who believed he could thus present an analysis of *average* European urine! Aside from physical and chemical, there are physiological averages, or what we might call average descriptions of phenomena, which are even more false. Let me assume that a physician collects a great many individual observations of a disease and that he makes an average description of symptoms observed in the individual cases; he will thus have a description that will never be matched in nature. So in physiology, we must never make average descriptions of experiments, because the true relations and phenomena disappear in the average; when dealing with complex and variable experiments, we must study their various circumstances, and then present our most perfect experiment as a type, which, however still stands for true facts. In the case just considered, averages must therefore be rejected, because they confuse, while aiming to unify, and distort while aiming to simplify. Averages are applicable only to reducing very slightly varying numerical data about clearly defined and *absolutely simple* cases.

A striking situation in which the use of averaged data provides "a description that will never be matched in nature" comes from the standard procedure of averaging data across individuals for each trial in learning experiments. As psychologists have only too recently realized * "the mean curve does not provide the information necessary to make statements concerning the function for the individual." It is perhaps easiest to illustrate this point with a hypothetical example.

Imagine a learning experiment where we flash ten letters before a subject and then ask him to repeat as many of these letters as he can, immediately after the flash. We record, for that trial, the number of letters he can correctly name. We continue with more trials until we have conducted, with each subject, a total of six trials. We are interested in employing these data to find how performance on this task increases as a function of number of trials. The following table presents a strictly hypothetical outcome for this experiment in terms of the data from four subjects:

Number of Correct Letters

	Trial					
Subject	1	2	3	4	5	6
1	0	10	10	10	10	10
2	0	0	10	10	10	10
3	0	0	0	10	10	10
4	0	0	0	0	10	10
Totals	0	10	20	30	40	40
Average	0	2.5	5.0	7.5	10.0	10.0

* See M. Sidman. A note on functional relations obtained from group data. *Psychol. Bull.*, 1952, 9, 263–269. Also, W. K. Estes. The problem of inference from curve based on group data. *Psychol. Bull.*, 1956, 53, 134–140.

The table represents each subject as jumping abruptly from getting none to getting all the letters correct. The only thing that varies from individual to individual is the trial on which this sudden jump takes place. Such complete all-or-none learning is probably not very likely in this kind of experiment, but the example serves to make the point under discussion vivid. Even if each subject mastered the task more gradually, but at a different rate from the others, the averaging procedure would still be likely to obscure the form of the learning curve in the manner illustrated below.

The graph in Figure 3, which plots the average number of correct letters as a function of trials, is one way in which the data from this experiment might be summarized. In fact, up until recent criticisms, this method of summarizing data from learning experiments was the standard practice. Many mathematical equations and theories of how learning takes place were based on these averaged group curves.

A reasonable interpretation of such a graph, one that is not implausible in terms of other research on learning, is that subjects master this task gradually; the learning curve, as such a graph is called, shows that mastery of the task proceeds in gradual and equal steps with each trial until the task is fully mastered by the fifth trial. However, if we interpreted this curve as a statement of how the "average" or typical subject mastered the task in this experiment it would be entirely false. As an examination of the hypothetical table of results shows, not one single subject learned the task in small steps. Every subject mastered it in one single trial, but subjects differed in the occurrence of this critical trial.

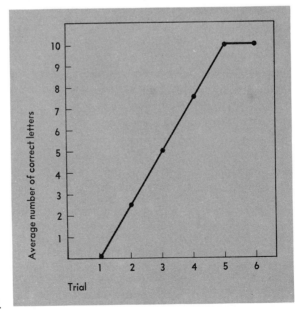

Figure 3.

Although this set of data was deliberately contrived to make the point easy to grasp, the fact that individual learning curves may rarely resemble the average curve for the group is now well recognized. Yet, as W. K. Estes, who has carefully examined the implication of this problem, points out: *

It is noteworthy that learning theory, even quantitative learning theory, has made rather steady progress in spite of the widespread acceptance of a false methodological assumption. Apparently inferences from averaged curves, although not necessarily correct, must in fact often be so. This being the case, researchers in learning are unlikely to give up readily the habit of computing mean curves of functional relationship. My purpose in this note is to show that we need not feel obliged to try. The group curve will remain one of our most useful devices both for summarizing information and for theoretical analysis *provided only that it is handled with a modicum of tact and understanding.*

Studies in which the differential method is employed to characterize one group as opposed to another seem especially to invite confusion between the group average and the individuals who constitute the group. It is tempting, after one has discovered that a group of exceptional students or creative architects differs from a comparison group on traits A, B, and C, to slip into the habit of talking about the results in terms of *the* creative person. Again, an artificial example will most easily dramatize this point. Assume we are studying a group of creative artists to discover whether such individuals have a typical personality pattern as measured by a set of ratings. Suppose that we employ ratings on two traits, "spontaneity" and "self-confidence," so that a rating of 0 is the average level of this trait in a comparison group, a rating of 1 is an indication of being above average, and a rating of 2 would indicate being very much above average. A set of ratings in our hypothetical and obviously oversimplified example might look like this for individuals in our "creative" group:

| Subject | Trait | |
	Spontaneity	Self-confidence
1	2	0
2	2	0
3	0	1
4	0	1
5	0	1
Total	4	3
Average	0.8	0.6

If in a large group of individuals, these averages, say, are found to be significantly different from those for the control group, we could then say, that the creative artists, as a group, tend to differ from the less creative artists

* W. K. Estes. The problem of inference from curves based on group data. *Psychol. Bull.*, 1956, 53, 134–140.

in being "spontaneous" and "self-confident." From the results of such an investigation you cannot know if this difference based on group averages reflects a pattern that is characteristic of any or even most of the individuals within the group. Such is the case with most studies based on individual differences where large numbers of comparisons or correlations are employed. Yet, it is all too easy—and all too common—to begin talking about *the* creative artist as being spontaneous and self-confident. This tendency to treat a profile based on group averages as a reflection of an individual's personality pattern, as you can see, is in principle the same mistake made with learning curves. In our example, we can readily see the mistake by looking at the profiles for individual subjects. No individual subject is characterized by the group profile; some individuals contribute to the high average on one trait, while different individuals contribute to the other part of the composite profile. For these data, a better summary, one that can be discovered only by an investigator who abandons the automatic and traditional methods of processing data that characterize such studies, would be to say that the creative individual in this study is one who is either spontaneous or self-confident, but not both.

ON STATISTICAL INFERENCE

In addition to becoming more aware of the fallacies and distortions that can arise from the misuse of averages and other summary statistics, statisticians and their customers have begun to re-examine the role that statistical inference does and should play in psychological inquiry. A very important way in which scientific inquiry advances our knowledge is in gradually eliminating alternative explanations of a given phenomenon. In a field such as psychology, where variation from one subject to another and from one response to the next is so marked, one alternative that must frequently be considered is that the results of any inquiry are due to chance. The introduction of the control group into psychological research at the turn of this century was a step in the direction of assessing the role of "chance," or coincidental factors, in a psychological experiment. The control condition served to provide an empirical *baseline,* or *standard,* against which to contrast the performance of subjects under an experimental or critical condition.

The introduction of statistical tests of significance, in the 1930's, took us a step further, giving us an *objective criterion* for deciding when an observed deviation from the standard could be attributed to factors other than chance. The significance test ritual aims at reducing the number of reports in which the results are merely coincidence. The test is set up to guard against "Type I errors," as they are called. These are errors we make when we conclude that a difference is real when it is in fact a matter of chance.

In the classical test for significance, as set up by R. A. Fisher, an investigator is allowed to make only one kind of decision. He can reject chance as an explanation. The test is so constructed that a big observed difference leads the investigator to reject the null hypothesis. If the difference is not larger than the critical value, the experimenter does not make a decision. He suspends judgment. Thus, the only mistake he can make is to reject chance when the results are actually due to chance. If he does this, he makes a Type I error. If his test fails to allow him to reject chance, then he can say nothing at all. He cannot say that his test, for example, supports the hypothesis of chance. All he can do, is merely report that he failed to reject chance.

Although this may strike you as hair-splitting, the question of what the failure to reject chance implies has resulted in big squabbles among statisticians. As a result of this controversy, a change was introduced among some, but still not all, users of statistical tests with the recognition of the possibility of a Type II error. This can occur when the psychologist accepts the hypothesis that chance produced his results when, in fact, the difference is actually "real." To oversimplify the matter somewhat, we can say that the Fisherian approach seems to treat the investigator as an individual who is too prone to see relationships where none exist. Hence, the test is set up to guard the investigator and the scientific community from the tendency to see relationships where only accident exists.

The newer position seems to express concern over the possibility that too much emphasis on avoiding chance results may result in overlooking important and real relationships (Type II error). In the new approach, the investigator has to consider the "power" of his test—its ability to "catch" a real effect if one is truly there.

The Role of Prior Information
in Statistical Inference

The statistical methods currently in use make most sense if we pretend that each experiment is evaluated without reference to previous experiments on the same topic. Imagine, for example, that a researcher decides to repeat Asch's experiment, but employs students in another country, say England. Suppose, for illustration's sake, that he uses 50 controls and 50 critical subjects and discovers that 58 per cent of the critical subjects, as compared with 42 per cent of the control subjects, make at least one error on the critical trials. Although this observed difference is in the expected direction, a standard statistical test will not allow the investigator to reject the hypothesis that the results are due to chance.

Although the Asch experiment has been replicated with consistent results in many different laboratories and many times, the statistical test is oblivious to the other experiments. It will give the investigator the same answer concerning the probability that the difference between 58 per cent and 42 per cent is a matter of chance whether this is the first time this experiment has been conducted or whether it is the one-thousandth time it has been conducted. Most investigators would have more confidence in this slight effect being real, regardless of the statistical test, if this were the Asch experiment, than they would have in, say, the reality of a much bigger and statistically significant outcome of an experiment that contradicts the results of previous research. Obviously there is a discrepancy between the uses of statistical inference and the way in which theories actually get accepted or rejected.

The current controversy among statisticians concerns the issue of how an investigator should employ his previous knowledge of a field when he makes a significance test. One school of thought argues for allowing the investigator to make use of his previous knowledge in the form of subjective estimates of the probability of various outcomes before the experiment. Then his observed result would be combined with the expectations to form a new estimate of the probabilities. The orthodox school, which opposes this idea, argues that the introduction of subjective probabilities into statistical testing removes the chief virtue of such tests—their objectivity and their independence of the individual's subjective beliefs. Again, we are confronted with the dilemma of choosing between objectivity and rigor, on the one hand, and subjectivity and relevance to "reality," on the other.

The misuse of averages and controversies over the proper role of statistical inference are only two of the symptoms of current uneasiness among many scientists in the biological and social sciences about where statistics belongs. Not too long ago, it was universally accepted that a psychologist was not capable of doing adequate research unless he had mastered the rudiments of statistical methodology. This belief is exhibited today in the fact that it is impossible to obtain a graduate degree in psychology at any major university without having the equivalent of at least a one-year course in statistics. But now the pendulum is beginning to swing the other way. There are signs of a reaction against the assumption that statistics is a necessary ingredient for acceptable psychological inquiry. Indeed, leading psychologists are asking whether an overemphasis on statistical methodology has resulted in inferior rather than superior research. Maybe, as one committee of psychologists has put it, it is true "that heavy emphasis on complex 'design of experiment' procedures at an early stage of training may give the student a false conception of the art of research and may tend to induce as well a kind of perfectionism that can act as a positive barrier to fertility or invention or flexibility of thinking." This committee adds, "Somehow the student must learn to find and use the methods appropriate to his problem—to avoid limiting his choice of problems to those which can be handled by methods with which he is familiar or by which he is overly impressed." * We should add that this committee, which was composed of eight of the most successful investigators in contemporary psychology, does not deny the necessity of statistical conceptions in the training for research. Rather, it wants to put statistical tools in their proper perspective. In its own words, "it is also quite clear that much that is important in research depends upon only the most elementary statistical conceptions; for such work overformalization and overelaboration of statistical tools can be a positive hindrance."

* L. Festinger *et al.* Education for research in psychology. *Amer. Psychol.,* 1959, 14, 167–179.

In this chapter we have touched on only a sampling of many issues concerning the description, analysis, and statistical evaluation of data. We could have profitably devoted time to matters involving how psychologists go about assigning numbers to psychological dimensions, to the implications of the assumption in almost all our data-reduction procedures that variables and psychological entities combine in a linear or additive manner, to the role and accessibility of high-speed computers and the consequent standardization of computational routines, to newer developments in multidimensional scaling and in statistical procedures designed to handle more realistically some of the problems that face the investigator, or to a host of other important matters that can affect the outcome of an inquiry.

Fortunately, when we step back and look at the controversies and disagreements that revolve around the use of measurement and statistics in psychology, we see that they are the same issues, in a slightly different guise, that confronted us when we considered the role of constraints and controls in collecting data or in designing investigations. Every scientific procedure for both collecting and describing data imposes some constraints on the form that the results can achieve. All scientific inquiry requires *selecting* only certain features of the environment for consideration, *abstracting* from these features only some of their attributes, and placing *constrictions* on the observer and the observed so that by *ignoring* or *holding constant* some features of the situation we can better see the relationships among other features.

When we recognize that all inquiry proceeds by ignoring some features of reality, we can better realize that many of the criticisms against the use of statistics and premature quantification in psychology are misplaced. It is not statistical tools as such that cause the trouble. Rather, it is the use of any tools or methods of inquiry without sufficient examination of their "credentials." What may be a perfectly adequate tool for one conceptual focus may become a "positive hindrance" for a later stage within the same inquiry or for a new question that arises as a result of the inquiry. An investigator may begin an investigation by applying factor analysis to a set of correlations. The resulting factors may raise some questions in his mind about the nature of these factors. If the same investigator pursues these questions by further application of factor analysis, rather than by subjecting his questions to more appropriate and different approaches, then he is no longer using factor analysis as a tool for inquiry. Rather, he has forsaken his original problem by becoming wedded to the tool. If sterile research results from this investigator's repeated reliance on one tool, this is not the fault of the tool of factor analysis in particular. Rather the fault lies in failing to fully grasp the nature of one's problem and the limitations of each tool. The only remedy is to try to keep ourselves oriented toward matching the constraints in the observational and processing procedures to the level and requirements of our research problems.

Interpreting the Data

"The first condition to be fulfilled by men of science, applying themselves to the investigation of natural phenomena, is to maintain absolute freedom of mind, based on philosophical doubt. Yet we must not be in the least sceptical; we must believe in science, i.e., in determinism; we must believe in a complete and necessary relation between things, among the phenomena proper to living things as well as in others; but at the same time we must be thoroughly convinced that we know this relation only in a more or less approximate way, and that the theories we hold are far from embodying changeless truths. When we propound a gen-

6

eral theory in our sciences we are sure only that, literally speaking, all such theories are false. They are only partial and provisional truths which are necessary to us, as steps on which we rest, so as to go on with investigation; they embody only the present state of our knowledge, and consequently they must change with the growth of science, and all the more often when sciences are less advanced in their evolution." (Claude Bernard, 1865.)

Any attempt to deal systematically with the role of interpretation within psychological theories would get us into the subject matter and history of psychology. And these latter topics are beyond the scope of this volume. Here, we simply want to discuss a few different approaches to the interpretation of data to illustrate how this phase of psychological inquiry interacts with the other phases and how it varies with the different developmental stages of an inquiry. My view of the role of interpretation, a view to which many contemporary psychologists would probably subscribe, is summed up in the words of one of our most eminent psychologists, Donald O. Hebb: "What we need from a theory is that it should hold together long enough to lead us to a better one." In the same article, Hebb describes how the earlier theories of Pavlov, Thorndike, and Watson, while being highly oversimplified, nevertheless "served the function of good theory by leading to their own destruction—they led to new analyses, new data, new ideas which in their turn make new theoretical formulations possible." * Note the similarity of this viewpoint to that expressed in the quotation from Bernard at the beginning of this chapter.

FORMAL VERSUS INFORMAL APPROACHES

Psychologists differ greatly among themselves concerning the applicability of formal theory to research on animal and human behavior. At one extreme was the late psychologist Clark Hull, who devoted much of his career to developing a rigorous, formal, deductive theory for all of human behavior. In reply to the question of whether psychology is ready for such a rigorous theory, Hull had this to say: †

No doubt many will feel that such standards of scientific theory may be suitable for theoretical physics, but that they are quite impossible in psychology, at least for the present. To take such a view is equivalent to holding that we can have no genuinely scientific theory in psychology. This is indeed conceivable, but if so we ought not to pretend to have theories at all. There are signs that the beginnings of a genuinely scientific theory of mammalian behavior are already on their way.

At the other extreme we find B. F. Skinner, who believes that at psychology's present stage of development the attempt to provide formal theories is

* D. O. Hebb. Alice in Wonderland or psychology among the biological sciences. In H. F. Harlow and C. N. Woolsey (eds.). *Biological and biochemical bases of behavior.* Madison: University of Wisconsin Press, 1958, pp. 451–467.

† C. L. Hull. Conflicting psychologies of learning—a way out. *Psychol. Rev.,* 1935, 42, 491–516.

premature. Indeed, he feels that formal theories can retard the development of psychological research. In an article written 15 years after Hull saw the "beginnings of a genuinely scientific theory" of behavior, Skinner raised two arguments against the use of theory in psychology.* First, Skinner believes that an emphasis on formalization may seduce us into forgetting our primary task of accounting for

behavior in its relation to certain manipulable variables; [instead,] we are likely to close our eyes to it and to use the theory to give us answers in place of the answers we might find through further study. It might be argued that the principal function of learning theory to date has been, not to suggest appropriate research, but to create a false sense of security, an unwarranted satisfaction with the *status quo.*

Skinner's second argument is that

research designed with respect to theory is also likely to be wasteful. That a theory generates research does not prove its value unless the research is valuable. Much useless experimentation results from theories, and much energy and skill are absorbed by them. Most theories are eventually overthrown, and the greater part of the associated research is discarded.

SKINNER ON SUPERSTITIOUS BEHAVIOR

Because it is easy to misinterpret what Skinner means by "theory," we shall begin our illustrations of how interpretation enters into psychological research by describing one of Skinner's own studies. We shall then follow the analysis of Skinner's approach to investigating and reporting on psychological phenomena with an extensive analysis of two other examples. By making such a detailed comparison, we not only should be in a better position to see how three outstanding psychologists approach the investigation and explanation of behavior from different viewpoints, but we should also be in a better position to sense the role that interpretation and explanation plays in all research.

In 1948 Skinner reported some interesting observations on what he referred to as "superstition" in the pigeon.† He introduced the study by "hypothesizing" that: "Whenever we present a state of affairs which is known to be reinforcing at a given drive, we must suppose that conditioning takes place, even though we have paid no attention to the behavior of the organism in making the presentation." To illustrate this generalization, he described the following experiment. A pigeon, which is kept in a hungry state by being maintained at 75 per cent of its normal body weight, is placed in a special cage for a few minutes each day. A mechanism presents food to the bird at regular intervals *with no reference whatsoever to the bird's behavior.* Since the pigeon is hungry and since food, under these conditions, is a "reinforcer,"

* B. F. Skinner. Are theories of learning necessary? *Psychol. Rev.,* 1950, 57, 193–216.
† B. F. Skinner. "Superstition" in the pigeon. *J. exp. Psychol.,* 1948, 38, 168–72.

we can expect, along with Skinner, that whatever the pigeon happens to be doing at the time the food is presented should be reinforced, or strengthened. In Skinner's "explanatory system," this means that the behavior occurring at the time the pigeon is given food will more likely occur again.

And that is exactly what did happen. At least it did in six out of the eight pigeons who were observed in this situation. One pigeon happened to be turning in a counterclockwise rotation when the food came. With repeated presentations of the food, this pattern of behavior developed into a conditioned response. Between reinforcements the pigeon would perform this counterclockwise "dance" two or three times until the food was presented again. Another bird developed "a 'tossing' response, as if placing its head beneath an invisible bar and lifting it repeatedly." The other birds who showed conditioning developed equally arbitrary patterns of behavior.

Skinner's explanation of this behavior is fairly straightforward.

The bird happens to be executing some response [i.e., activity] as the hopper (which presents the food) appears; as a result it tends to repeat this response. If the interval before the next presentation is not so great that extinction takes place, a second "contingency" is probable. This strengthens the response still further and subsequent reinforcement becomes more probable. It is true that some responses go unreinforced and some reinforcements appear when the response has not just been made, but the net result is the development of a considerable state of strength.

Drawing on his previous experience with this kind of conditioning as well as additional observations made in the present situation, Skinner adds further explanations and makes some concrete predictions about what would happen, say, if the interval between arbitrary reinforcements were lengthened or shortened. One generalization (which other more theoretically minded psychologists would call a testable hypothesis) is that, as the interval between food presentations is made shorter, conditioning should be speedier and more obvious. One basis for this "deduction" is that, as time passes after reinforcement, a pigeon is more and more likely to drift into other behavior; it would therefore be less likely to be repeating its first response when the food comes a second time. A related reason is that as the time interval increases the pigeon is also less likely to be in the same part of the cage the second time the food is presented. If the time interval between reinforcements becomes very short, Skinner even predicts what the nature of the conditioned response will be. "In the limiting case of a very brief interval the behavior to be expected would be holding the head toward the opening through which the magazine [food dispenser] has disappeared."

Skinner is able to make further speculations concerning what would happen under different levels of drive, under gradually increasing intervals between reinforcements, and with the termination of reinforcements. In these latter cases, he is able to describe further observations that support his generalizations.

Although Skinner avoids setting down his results in the guise of a formal theory, he does not hesitate, after a fashion, to use his highly controlled experiment on pigeons to suggest possible "explanations" of superstition as it occurs at the human level under nonlaboratory conditions. In his own words:

> The experiment might be said to demonstrate superstition. The bird behaves as if there were a causal relation between its behavior and the presentation of food, although such a relation is lacking. There are many analogies in human behavior. Rituals for changing one's luck at cards are good examples. A few accidental connections between a ritual and favorable consequences suffice to set up and maintain the behavior in spite of many unreinforced instances. The bowler who has released a ball down the alley but continues to behave as if he were controlling it by twisting and turning his arm and shoulder is another case in point. These behaviors have, of course, no real effect upon one's luck or upon a ball half way down an alley, just as in the present case the food would appear as often if the pigeon did nothing—or, more strictly speaking, did something else.

We can now better grasp what Skinner means when he takes a stand against theories. Skinner obviously *does* theorize in some meanings of that term. He generalizes beyond his immediate results. He makes predictions on the basis of these generalizations. He states his expectations concerning what would happen if the interval were shortened, if drive were increased, if different intervals were employed on the same bird, and so on. These predictions or expectations can be checked by gathering further data. When the new data conflict with his expectations, he revises these expectations and changes his generalizations. Because he deliberately avoids stating and testing formal hypotheses, Skinner may achieve greater flexibility in adapting his expectations and observations to immediate feedback from each new item of information. On the other hand, Skinner's failure to formalize his system makes it difficult, if not impossible, for him to convey to his readers the actual basis for his generalizations and the reasons for his choice of one variable rather than another in making new observations.

Skinner also does not hesitate to employ his results to help us "understand" behavior of human beings in more complex situations. He employs his pigeon experiment as a model for certain kinds of human rituals and superstitions. The actual testing of this application of the model is impossible within Skinner's framework.

Yet it is clear that Skinner is against the use of models in psychological inquiry when they are employed in another form. He has been consistently against attempts by other psychologists to "explain" behavior of organisms in neurological terms. In fact, the kind of theory that Skinner is against is the kind that uses theoretical terms, such as "synapses," "neurones," or "connections"—terms that are on a conceptual level different from the observed behavior for which the experimenter wants to account.

So here is one approach to the interpretation of data. Skinner is unwilling to jump from the pigeon's food-oriented behavior to the pigeon's brain, but, within his system, he is willing to jump from the pigeon's behavior to the superstitious rituals of people in card games and at the bowling alley.

Now let us look at a psychologist whose conceptual focus, in contrast to Skinner's position, is oriented towards explaining an animal's food-related behavior in terms of physiological mechanisms in the brain. Psychologists, including Skinner, have relied heavily on controlling the motivation of their subjects by depriving them of food or water and thereby setting up a hunger or thirst drive. Hunger and thirst have also played leading theoretical roles in psychology as examples of two of the primary, or basic, drives. Until only recently these two drives have served as models for many of the leading theories of motivation, especially in the area of learning theory.

Today it is pretty clear that the brain plays a key role in eating and drinking behavior. It is with one psychologist's attempt to discover the role of the brain in eating behavior that we shall now concern ourselves. For details of this illustration I shall rely on Philip Teitelbaum's masterful summary of his own contributions, as well as those of other psychologists, towards the unraveling of this mystery.*

A convenient starting point for the present inquiry is Froelich's observation at the turn of the century of a person with a tumor of the pituitary gland who became obese. Other observations had been made prior to this time which suggested that tumors in this area of the brain went along with obesity. Because the pituitary gland is closely associated anatomically with a part of the brain known as the hypothalamus, controversy soon arose over whether the obesity was due to lesions of the pituitary gland or to lesions in the hypothalamus. In the 1920's a series of studies on dogs and rats settled the controversy. P. E. Smith, for example, showed that if the pituitary was carefully removed without damaging the hypothalamus, a rat would not become fat. On the other hand, if the hypothalamus were damaged, a rat would become obese. As Teitelbaum points out,

these experiments were a landmark for two reasons. First, they showed that one could produce the phenomenon experimentally in animals, thus opening the way for precise localization in the brain, and for the experimental study of the phenomenon under controlled conditions in the laboratory. Second, they completely eliminated pituitary damage as the cause of this form of obesity and pointed to the hypothalamus as the part of the brain that was involved.

The hypothalamus is a very small, relatively inaccessible cluster of cells at the base of the brain. The work that finally led to its isolation as the organ involved in obesity took great care and skill. But, even so, further investigation demanded more reliable and precise ways of making lesions in this part

* P. Teitelbaum. Disturbances in feeding and drinking behavior after hypothalamic lesions. In M. Jones (ed.). *Nebraska symposium on motivation, 1961*. Lincoln: University of Nebraska Press, copyright 1961, pp. 36–69. All quotations in this account reprinted by permission of University of Nebraska Press.

of the brain without simultaneously involving other parts. In the 1930's an instrument, originally invented in 1905, was refined and adapted to the problem. This device, called the stereotaxic instrument, enabled physiologists to make precise, minute bilateral lesions in different parts of the rat's hypothalamus. With this major technological improvement, investigators could now attempt to pinpoint the effects of damage in different areas of this very small, but important part of the brain.

With this new-found precision, investigators discovered that damage to one part of the hypothalamus produced obesity. But lesions just slightly to the side of this area produced an opposite effect. The animal would cease to eat and starve to death.

The next big step towards the goal of explaining this obesity was a behavioral observation. In 1943 three physiologists made the simple, but important, observation that the rats who had these hypothalamic lesions became obese because they were eating much more than normal animals. They called this phenomenon hypothalamic hyperphagia (the word hyperphagia consists of two Greek roots meaning overeating). That this physiological effect has behavioral manifestations, of course, suggests that psychologists, who concentrate on behavior, as well as physiologists could become interested in this overeating activity. And, as it has turned out, the further investigation of hypothalamic hyperphagia has been a cooperative effort between physiologists and psychologists—the one group contributing its anatomical and surgical skills, the other group contributing its techniques for controlling and measuring behavioral effects.

The first explanation that occurred to the physiologists was that the overeating was due to a disturbance of the rat's metabolism. But a series of experiments showed, among other things, that if one of the hypothalamic rats was starved it lost weight at a normal rate. This indicated that the rat was able to use its own fat reserves in the same way a normal rat does. Consequently, the evidence ruled out the possibility of metabolic disturbance as a causal factor.

A variety of evidence also led Teitelbaum to eliminate two other explanations. A "thermostatic" theory, for example, suggested that the overeating was connected with an impairment in the rat's ability to detect differences in temperature. And a "glucostatic" theory suggested that damage to the hypothalamic cells altered the level of glucose in the blood. Both direct and indirect considerations eliminated these proposals.

Teitelbaum began his inquiry by first taking a closer look at the actual eating behavior of the rats. In what way did an operated rat actually differ from a normal rat? Note that the question, put at this level, is a psychological question rather than a physiological one. Does a rat, for example, try to regulate the amount it eats in terms of the number of calories in the food, that is, the amount of nutritive value? Or does it eat for bulk? There was already evidence at hand, for example, which indicated that a normal rat tries to take in a fixed amount of calories. If you dilute his food with a nonnutritive substance like cellulose, the rat will eat more food to get his usual amount of calories. Even when the diet is 75 per cent cellulose, the rat will attempt to increase the bulk of the food it ingests to keep its caloric intake at a constant level. Will the hyperphagic rat do likewise?

With a normal diet, a hyperphagic rat will increase its food intake to as much as four times its normal amount. Once the operated rat reaches a weight of about twice its normal body weight, it still continues to eat as much as twice what a normal rat will consume in one day. But with even a slight adulteration in its diet, Teitelbaum found that this dramatic pattern of over-eating was strikingly reversed. In fact, if the operated rat's diet is adulterated with as little as 25 per cent cellulose (an amount that leads a normal rat to eat more food) it will stop eating almost entirely. The picture presents itself of a rat that will voraciously stuff itself with a normal diet, but will starve for as long as a full week rather than eat food that is slightly altered from the normal diet.

Teitelbaum guessed that the rat was reacting with special sensitivity to certain stimuli in the food. When he added a slight amount of a bitter substance, such as quinine, to the diet of a normal rat, the rat ate as much as usual. But even with an amount as small as one part in 800, the hyperphagic rat refused to eat the adulterated diet. Conversely, when a similarly minute amount of a sweet substance was added to the diet, the normal rat did not eat more, but the operated rat ate much more.

If a psychologist observes that a rat eats more food than would be normally expected, he is likely to conclude that the rat's motivation for food has increased. And it was natural to look upon the effect of this hypothalamic operation as somehow increasing the rat's motivation for eating. Yet, when he considered that the operated rat would stop eating if the palatability of its diet were even slightly altered, and when he reviewed some previous experimental evidence, Teitelbaum speculated that maybe the reverse of this first impression was true. Maybe the operation impairs rather than increases the rat's motivation for food. An experiment confirmed this expectation. The operated rats eat more than normal rats when the food is easily accessible and palatable. But when it is required that they exert some effort to acquire food pellets, the hyperphagic rats will not work as hard as the normal rat. "So even though hyperphagic rats overeat, they do not seem hungrier. Motivation for food is, if anything, weaker than in the normal rat."

Investigating the eating behavior of the operated rats further, Teitelbaum discovered that the hyperphagic rats do not overeat by eating more frequently, but by eating larger meals when they do eat. Once they start to eat a meal, they do not show satiation as quickly as do normal rats. By experimenting and thinking about this phenomenon in more detail, the investigator decided that the operated rats eat to regulate the caloric content of their food. This conclusion directly reverses the one from Teitelbaum's first experiment where he apparently demonstrated that operated rats do not regulate the nutritive content of their diet. This reversal of an earlier conclusion, a common feature of research, came about through the realization that the first experiment actually pitted together two opposing determinants of the rat's eating behavior—the altered palatability of the diet as well as its altered caloric intake. When these two factors are separately manipulated, it turns out that a rat will increase its food when the caloric value is decreased as long as the palatability of the diet is not impaired. The first experiment, then, had masked this effect.

Although the work up to this point had eliminated some possible explanations and had added new factors to the picture, the intensive probing of what had begun as a relatively direct correlation between a brain center and eating was pointing to a complex and seemingly confused picture. Such a stage is also quite typical of intensive investigation into psychological phenomena. At this stage Teitelbaum describes the situation as follows:

These results compose a puzzling picture of animals that overeat but do not display increased hunger, and that regulate their caloric intake at about twice the normal level, but are so sensitive to the palatability of the diet that regulation is often prevented by a slightly negative taste of the food.

Rephrasing the Problem

Sometimes what apparently seem to be impassable barriers in the way of further progress on a scientific problem are suddenly broken down or circumvented by a slightly different way of asking the original question. One of the most famous and striking examples is Einstein's struggle with the problem of what happens to an observer when he is in motion relative to the velocity of light. Max Wertheimer has given us an excellent account of the stages of development in Einstein's thinking as he struggled with this problem for a period of seven years prior to the formulation of his special theory of relativity.* Einstein first began work on the problem when he was 16 years old. He wondered, what would happen if you run after a ray of light? If you ride on its beam? If you run after the beam, does its velocity decrease? For seven years, Einstein brooded and puzzled over these questions. Throughout this period he tried to solve the problem within the classical framework of physics. He kept trying to work out the answer, for example, by treating the velocity of light as a variable within Maxwell's system. But something was always wrong; things just did not seem to fit together. Then, after seven years of brooding over the problem, Einstein rephrased his question by focusing on how one can measure the velocity of light from a moving position as compared with the position of a stationary observer. With this new formulation, what had been an intractable problem, became transformed into the special theory of relativity within a matter of five weeks.

In the present example, although we may not be dealing with anything

* M. Wertheimer. *Productive thinking.* Enlarged ed. New York: Harpers, 1959.

as world-shaking as relativity, the principle still holds that a rephrasing of the question or a slight shift in focus often opens up new ways to grasp a phenomenon. The initial and most striking aspect of a hyperphagic rat is the fact that he overeats. Consequently, it is quite natural to focus attention on this eating—what starts it going? But the new turn in the quest for understanding this phenomenon came when the focus was shifted from the eating to the cessation of eating. In Teitelbaum's words:

My own belief, as far as the phenomenon of hypothalamic hyperphagia is concerned, is that the important clue to the nature of the deficit is not that the animals overeat, but that they stop overeating when their weight has reached a new high plateau. The defect is in their weight regulation, not in their regulation of food intake; if this is corect, then one might say that the hyperphagic rat overeats to get fat. Once it is fat, it no longer overeats."

The new formulation now calls attention to what it is that keeps the operated rat at a different weight level from that of the normal rat. An immediate possibility is that somehow the rat's eating is controlled by his weight. When his weight reaches a certain level, he stops eating. This feedback control of amount of eating would be true for normal and operated rats. The difference between the two rats, on this new hypothesis, is that the operation somehow changes the optimum weight the rat attempts to maintain.

From this new speculation Teitelbaum was able to deduce testable consequences. "Then it follows that if a rat was already obese, it would not overeat after hypothalamic lesions. And if a normal rat was induced to overeat by some temporary means and become obese, then after the cause of its overeating was removed, it should eat much less until its weight returned to a normal level." The experiments carried out to test this hypothesis confirmed the expectations. Teitelbaum artificially increased the eating of normal rats by injections of insulin. After their weight was raised to the level that would be achieved by a hyperphagic rat, some of these rats were then operated upon and the others were used as controls. When the insulin injections were stopped, the control rats cut down their eating until their weight was back to normal. The operated rats, on the other hand, did not overeat, but, rather, ate just enough to keep themselves at pre-operative weight, which had already been artificially boosted. Teitelbaum quotes a colleague who suggested that "the animal must be constantly weighing itself."

Each answer to an experimental question always raises many more. By a series of ingenious experiments, which progressively eliminated one alternative after another, Teitelbaum has suggested why the operation affects a rat's eating behavior. It changes the weight-level the rat tries to maintain. But how is this reaction to weight accomplished? How does the rat go about "weighing" itself? What cues does it use? Again the search goes on. Teitelbaum assumes that the cells of the hypothalamic nucleus are receptors responding to "something" that is correlated with obesity. Several possibilities can exist. One is that a hormonal-like substance related to the rat's fat deposits circulates in the bloodstream. In a normal rat, the cells in the hypothalamus become active when a certain level of this substance is circulating; these activated cells then act, through the nervous system, to inhibit eating behavior. In the operated rat, many of these cells have been destroyed. Therefore, it takes a larger amount of this fat-correlated substance in the bloodstream to activate the receptors in the hypothalamus and cause inhibition of eating.

Teitelbaum warns us that several of the steps in his argument are, as yet, highly speculative and based on incomplete evidence. And, as he puts it:

A great deal of careful work must be done before we can really accept these views. But if they are correct, the problem of hypothalamic hyperphagia will boil down to a hunt for the hormone that acts on the cells in the ventromedial region of the hypothalamus to curb obesity.

This example shows how each experiment, in a chain of experiments, grew out of attempts to interpret and make sense out of the prior ones. Early in the inquiry, the conceptual focus became a matter of relating events at one conceptual level—the neurological—to events at another conceptual level—the behavioral. The quest centered around a striking phenomenon. A small lesion in a previously little-explored part of the brain resulted in dramatic, visible changes in an organism. When investigators in the late 1930's demonstrated how this effect could be reliably produced in the laboratory, the search for an explanation began. At first the explanation was sought for entirely in physiological terms—metabolic factors affecting an animal's utilization of fat deposits. Psychologists entered the scene when a physiologist happened to look at what the operated animal does and noticed that he eats more. For the psychologist the pursuit was to find neurological determinants of "motivated" behavior. An analysis of the animal's behavior was employed to gain further clues about the nature of the physiological mechanisms. It was a psychological discovery, in terms of behavior, which guided the physiological search. The behavioral evidence indicated that the rat regulates its eating to keep a constant weight. This psychological evidence now focused the physiological problem on the quest for a humoral substance in the blood that can be the direct stimulus activating the eating cells in the hypothalamus.

To gain an insight into the role of explanation and interpretation in psychological inquiry, we can inquire what it was that led Teitelbaum to focus on the stimulus, or palatability, aspects of the animal's diet. This development, which was a key turning point in the investigation, could derive from the intellectual climate in which Teitelbaum began his study. In this climate, the emphasis is on what is called a *central-motive-state* theory of motivation. This view is opposed to the once widely prevalent local-factors theory.* According to the central-motive-state theory, the hunger drive would stem not from any single local stimulus, such as stomach contractions, but, rather,

* See E. Stellar. The physiology of motivation. *Psychol. Rev.*, 1954, 61, 5–22.

from the combination of influences from sensory, hormonal, and neural factors. With this new theory as a guide, it was natural for the investigator to look for sensory as well as neural controls of the eating behavior. It seems unlikely that a physiologist, working under the old framework, which was established by Walter B. Cannon, would have thought of examining the palatability of the rat's diet as a factor in the overeating syndrome. And, of course, we would not expect a psychologist brought up under Skinner's orientation to attempt to explain eating behavior by reference to things going on in the animal's skull.

HEBB ON THE CONCEPTUAL NERVOUS SYSTEM

Our third case history represents, more than does the previous one, the kind of theorizing that Professor Skinner claims can lead to wasteful and valueless research. Skinner especially questions the appropriateness of theories that refer to events taking place in what he calls "the conceptual nervous system." Such events are taking place at a different level and within a different conceptual framework from those that the psychologist is trying to predict. In Skinner's view such conceptual constructs represent unnecessary middlemen. Almost as if in direct reply to Skinner, the psychologist Hebb entitled one of his addresses "Drives and the C. N. S. (Conceptual Nervous System)." * In this address, Hebb shows how his own conceptions of motivation have gradually been changed both in conformity with experimental evidence and in terms of new conceptions of the nervous system. Hebb's theorizing employs what psychologists call hypothetical constructs—theoretical entities that presumably could refer to actual and observable structures. Hebb's theoretical terms are constructs like synaptic knobs, cell assemblies, and phase sequences, all of which might plausibly turn out to have real physiological counterparts. Using such terms, Hebb has constructed a theory † that has been extremely productive in new research in both the physiology and the psychology of learning and motivation.

Our analysis of the development of Hebb's ideas on motivation will reveal how an interpretative approach condemned by Skinner can profitably serve as a model for continually adjusting our ideas about one domain of behavior.

By the time that an objective, behavioristic psychology began to attack the problem of why animals behave as they do, it was natural to emulate the approach of physics and chemistry and seek for the causes of action outside of the object rather than inside of it. Consequently, in the prevailing doctrine of motivation in American psychology up until the 1930's, an animal or human being was regarded as passive unless acted upon by external forces. The analogy, almost certainly influenced by the Industrial Revolution, was

---

* D. O. Hebb. *Psychol. Rev.*, 1955, 62, 243–254.
† D. O. Hebb. *Organization of behavior*. New York: Wiley, 1949.

that an organism is like a machine that operates only when it is supplied with power from a separate source. These sources of power or "drive" were held to be the so-called primary drives of hunger, sex, thirst, pain, and mothering. Other instigations to behavior such as seeking status, power, money and the like were seen as deriving by association from these more fundamental drives.

As Hebb points out, this conception of motivation was supported in the minds of psychologists by their conception of the nervous system as being inert unless activated from the outside. The early studies of nerve fibers, for example, indicated that they are inert until set off from the outside. This overly simple notion of motivation has persisted to the present day within psychology, Hebb implies, because many psychologists, even those who openly repudiate using the nervous system as a model, actually are still influenced by this outdated conception of the nervous system. It is not the attempt to use the nervous system as a model that interferes with contemporary theorizing, but the use of the wrong model—a model that has been abandoned by neurologists.

Even from the start, this stimulus-response conception of external drive was confronted with obvious difficulties. Animals were active when none of the primary drives seemed to be acting. They appeared to learn things about their environment and to seek and explore new situations even when they were not hungry or thirsty. The advocates of the predominant stimulus-response concept, however, handled these apparent exceptions in one of two ways. Some added the concept of acquired, or learned, drives to supplement the inborn, or primary, drives; some admitted the existence of additional basic motives such as activity and exploratory drives.

Here we come across an interesting illustration of how explanatory systems are "saved" or retained in the face of contradictory or challenging data. Unlike the stereotype that many textbooks convey, a scientist does not eagerly or willingly change his explanatory conceptions in the face of contradictory evidence. He attempts to salvage his theory by at least three expedients.

In the first place, he will try to deny that the apparent exceptions are really exceptions at all. When animals seem to learn in the absence of a primary drive, the results are inconclusive because it is difficult, if not impossible, to be really sure that all of the animals' primary needs for sex, food, water, and avoidance of pain are really at zero-level.

In the second place, the theorist may add supplementary principles or hypotheses to his original system. Thus, the advocate of classical drive theory can admit the existence of an exploratory drive to account for an animal's learning in a new situation and thereby save the rest of the system as well as the notion of external causes. Or he can add the idea of learned, or acquired, drives and so explain an animal's willingness to run a maze for novel stimulation as a secondary drive that derives its force from previous association of novel stimuli with obtaining food.

A third expedient is for the investigator to confine himself to types of inquiry or phenomena that best fit his conception. Hebb cites a number of easily accessible phenomena that, in retrospect, were well known and embarrassing to the dominant drive-conception during the first half of the twentieth century. He suggests that "we may overlook the rather large number of forms of behavior in which motivation cannot be reduced to biological drive plus learning. Such behavior is most evident in higher species, and may be forgotten by those who work only with the rat or with restricted segments of the behavior of dog or cat."

But despite the confinement of many psychologists to specific observational conditions, information began accumulating from a variety of sources until psychology as a whole was forced to come to grips with these apparent exceptions to the classical concept of drive. By the time of World War II, and thereafter, more and more psychologists were willing to admit the existence of a class of exploratory-activity drives. For Hebb, at least, this attempt to save motivational theory by simply appending more and more drives was dissatisfying. "We must not multiply drives beyond reason, and at this point one asks whether there is no alternative to the theory in this form."

The alternative that Hebb adopted was based on a newer conception of the central nervous system that developed around 1930. The nerve cell, it seems, actually is not physiologically inert when it is not being stimulated externally. It is active on its own account and can discharge without stimulation. "The nervous system is alive, and living things by their nature are active." In his new theory, Hebb gradually saw that the problem was not to account for the energizing of behavior but rather for its direction. In the earlier view, hunger was seen as a drive that arouses an animal to action. In the newer version, the animal is already active. Hunger is no longer a drive; it does not prod the animal into action. Instead it is a cue that guides or directs the animal's behavior into one kind of activity rather than another. If the rat is hungry his activity will be focused on food-getting. If he is not hungry he will be just as active, but he will focus on some other kind of activity.

Here we see how rephrasing a question, or refocusing our interest, can be a turning point both for theorizing and for guiding further research. We noted how Teitelbaum made a breakthrough in his study of overeating by changing the question from what makes the animal eat to what makes him *stop* eating. We see a striking parallel in the development of Hebb's theory of motivation. Hebb, at that point in his development, held that the human brain is "built to be active, and that as long as it is supplied with adequate nutrition [it] will continue to be active. Brain activity is what determines behavior, and so the only behavioral problem becomes that of accounting for *in*activity."

This new conceptual framework appeared to account for a lot of behavior that previously did not fit into motivational theory. It made sense, for example, out of the data Hebb had obtained in an earlier experiment. In this experiment all the students in a large school were told that they no longer were required to work unless they wanted to. If they made noise and interrupted other children at work, their "punishment" would be to be sent outside to play; the reward for being good was to do more work. "In these circumstances, *all* of the pupils discovered within a day or two that, within limits, they preferred work to no work (and incidentally learned more arithmetic and so forth than in previous years)."

Effects of Sensory Deprivation
on Hebb's Theory

Although this new viewpoint toward motivation helped to tie together more data about human behavior, some new experimental evidence soon convinced Hebb that he should revise his conception of motivation once again. The key experiment that raised the doubts in Hebb's mind was conducted by three psychologists in his department at McGill University.* In this experiment, a student was paid to lie on a bed in a small room for 24 hours a day, with time out for eating and going to the toilet. Each subject wore translucent goggles, gloves and cardboard cuffs, and every effort was made to prevent auditory or other sensory stimulation. In other words, within the limits of feasibility and ordinary comfort, the experimenters attempted to create a situation where each subject could spend a long period of time with no sensory input. Although the students were paid 20 dollars a day, which was double what they could earn on other jobs, and although they were encouraged to remain in the experiment as long as they wanted, very few subjects were willing to remain in this condition for more than a few days. The experiment soon became a classic and opened up a whole new line of research on the topic of sensory deprivation.

For Hebb, the experiment was a fatal blow to his theory of motivation. Although the subjects were well paid and were asked essentially to do nothing, they enjoyed the experiment only for from four to eight hours. Beyond this limit, they became increasingly restless, developed a strong need for stimulation, showed signs of disorganization, and revealed other symptoms of psychological impairment. Hebb asked himself:

If the thought process is internally organized and motivated, why should it break down in conditions of perceptual isolation, unless emotional disturbance intervenes? . . . The subjects were reasonably well adjusted, happy, and able to think coherently for the first four or five hours of the experiment; why, according, to my theory, should this not continue, and why should the organization of behavior not be promptly restored with restoration of the normal environment?

In an effort to find answers to his questions, Hebb once again turned to the latest findings of brain physiology to see if they could offer him some clues.

* W. H. Bexton, W. Heron, and T. H. Scott. Effects of decreased variation in the sensory environment. *Canad. J. Psychol.*, 1954, 8, 70–76.

One important clue was the discovery in the brain stem of an "arousal system." During the first half of this century, the classical conception was developed that sensory input from the receptors—such as eye, ear, nose, and touch receptors—made its way by relatively efficient and direct sensory pathways to the sensory areas of the cortex. The new conception suggests that sensory input actually travels to the cortex by two different pathways. One pathway is the classical one leading to the sensory cortex. This route is efficient and leads to relatively localized stimulation of parts of the brain. The second route for the incoming sensory input is by way of the arousal system in the brain stem. The incoming stimulation to the brain stem results in a diffuse, nonspecific stimulation of the cortex. Whereas the stimulation coming to the cortex by the main sensory pathways provides the organism with specific, qualitative information, the stimulation that reaches the cortex through the second, nonspecific pathway does not provide information. Rather it serves to tone up the cortex, to arouse it, to alert it for action. In fact, in experiments where this second pathway is surgically blocked, the animal becomes permanently inert and enters a coma.

Hebb conceptualizes these new findings in terms of their implication for psychology by suggesting that "we can now distinguish two quite different effects of a sensory event. One is the *cue function,* guiding behavior; the other, less obvious but no less important, is the *arousal* or *vigilance function.* Without a foundation of arousal, the cue function cannot exist." Hebb sees the arousal function as the equivalent of the energizing function of drive in the earlier stimulus-response formulations. So, in a sense, both empirical findings from psychological research and the newer physiological evidence of an arousal system bring Hebb back to the earlier conception of drive as an energizer of behavior. The newer conception, however, is a much more sophisticated version of the earlier theory of external motivation. It incorporates the stimulus-response model; but it also includes many phenomena that could not be handled by the earlier model. The new theory suggests that drive, or motivation, can either facilitate or impair performance. Low motivation results in poor performance; high motivation also can result in poor performance. This suggests that there is an optimal level of motivation for different types of tasks. For well-practiced and simple tasks, the higher the drive the better the performance. For example, if we are studying speed of running away from a noxious stimulus, then we would expect the speed to increase with the degree of painfulness of the stimulus. Even with such a straightforward task, however, if the arousal becomes extreme, paralysis induced by fear can result. On the other hand, if we are observing a more delicate task such as threading a needle, even a moderate amount of arousal might impair performance.

An even more interesting implication of this conception is the so-called discrepancy hypothesis. This hypothesis suggests that for any situation, an organism is motivated to seek an optimal amount of stimulation or arousal. If the incoming stimulation follows a pattern of complete expectation it does not serve to arouse or stimulate the individual. Hebb and others, for example, have used such a notion to explain why so-called popular music does not remain popular for very long. With repetition it no longer produces novel or unexpected stimulation. On the other hand, if the incoming stimulation is too chaotic and novel, then it will result in a level of activation beyond the optimal. This is why, for example, a modern composition in music, reaching the ears for the first time of one used to music of the Romantic period, can sound repulsive and annoying. The new conception suggests that individuals will constantly seek some deviation from what they are used to, but will avoid too much deviation.

With this new conception, Hebb feels that drive theory can now account, for the first time, for such things as the positive attraction that risk-taking and thrill-seeking seem to have for human beings. "This taste for excitement *must* not be forgotten when we are dealing with human motivation. It appears that, up to a certain point, threat and puzzle have positive motivating value, beyond that point negative value."

Of course, the new conception raises many problems. It, too, has inconsistencies and apparent contradictions to resolve. But its value lies in its ability to tie together phenomena that fitted into the older conceptions along with phenomena that did not fit so well. Moreover, the conception suggests a series of new empirical observations that can be made to clarify it as well as to test its implications. Already, a wide variety of experimentation owes its instigation to this new conception of the role of drive and cue in motivation. But this is the way explanation "works" within the process of inquiry.

THE VALUE OF THEORIES

Although Skinner feels that his approach is more likely to lead to valuable research, and that approaches such as Hebb's will lead to wasteful and useless research, Skinner has avoided the obviously sticky issue of specifying how we decide whether research is valuable or not. But we probably would have little or no dissent among most psychologists if we said that research generated by both Skinner's approach and Hebb's theory have contributed significantly to the advance of modern psychological inquiry. Skinner argues, as we saw, that "Most theories are eventually overthrown, and the greater part of the associated research is discarded." The evidence, at least as put together by historians of science in other scientific fields, seems to contradict Skinner's contention. Most theories are eventually overthrown, as Skinner maintains, but the research which they generated often survives and becomes incorporated and reinterpreted within succeeding theories. Following are some obvious examples. The Copernican system did not discard the data of Ptolemy, but merely rearranged them. Tycho Brahe's hybrid compromise between Copernicus and Ptolemy was overthrown by Kepler, but in so doing, Kepler retained and used all of Brahe's carefully collected data. The phlogiston theory of combustion, among other things, led to the discovery of oxygen. When Lavoisier overthrew it, he did not discard the various experimental data which it had generated; he incorporated all of them within the new system.

Although the scientific history of psychology is rather short, there is no reason to doubt the value and usefulness of much data that was collected under what we now consider faulty or discarded theories. All of Fechner's painfully gathered data on perception, for example, still form part of the basis of any of the current attempts to "repeal" Fechner's law, which states that sensation varies with the logarithm of the amount of physical stimulation, and replace it with something else. The volume of research that came out of Hull's attempt to set up a formal system based on Pavlov and the Law of Effect still forms part of the empirical basis which any new theory has to take into account. Pavlov's theory, especially its physiological aspects, has been completely ignored, but no psychologist, including Skinner himself, would consider Pavlov's experimental findings valueless. In fact, no modern theory of learning would succeed if it failed to fully incorporate all of Pavlov's experimental findings.

Whatever makes research valuable, whatever makes the difference between inquiries that succeed and those that fail, it seems clear that the essential ingredient does not reside in the nature of the explanatory system that guides the researcher in his inquiry and in his interpretations of the results. Skinner has clearly demonstrated that he, within the framework he espouses, can produce significant and important data. Hebb, Teitelbaum, Hull, the Gestalt psychologists, Watson, and other psychologists with different tastes and notions about the "proper" way to build theoretical systems, have all made important and valuable contributions in the form of key experiments that now form models for future generations of psychological investigators.

On the other hand, it seems equally evident that, in the hands of other psychologists, the approach of Skinner, or of Hebb, or of Watson, or of some other systematist, can result in trivia and irrelevancies that attempt to gain status by aping the terms or approach of the masters. Skinner and other psychologists who see wastefulness in various theoretical frameworks for inquiry are understandably reacting to these unfortunately unproductive research efforts. But Skinner may be missing the mark in trying to make theory or a particular type of explanatory approach the scapegoat. Trivia and useless research can emerge from almost any type of explanatory approach. Conversely, good research and important contributions can also emerge from these same approaches. Whatever the secret "ingredient" is, if there is one, it doesn't seem to reside in the particular terms the investigator prefers to employ or the degree of systematization he desires to embrace.

PSYCHOLOGICAL VERSUS LOGICAL NECESSITY FOR THEORIES

The discussion and illustrations in this chapter convey many different features concerning the role of interpretation in psychological inquiry. One important distinction is that between the *logical* role and the *psychological* role of explanatory systems.

From a *psychological* viewpoint, the role of explanation and interpretation raises several issues. For one thing, although models and visualizable interpretations of a theory are logically unnecessary, they may be psychologically necessary in at least two senses. It may be that on the road to the construction of a scientific theory, an individual scientist has to progress first through the medium of "mental models" (imagery, feelings, intuitions), then by way of explicit, communicable models (neurology, robots, mechanical and other analogies, until finally, at an advanced stage, he can remove these mental props and employ formal symbolism to display the finished system or theory. Secondly, although the formal theory logically includes all its consequences, which can be brought out by applying the rules of logic to the basic postulates of the system, logical consequences of many theories do not become *psychologically* apparent for most individuals until they employ a model to interpret the theory. In this case, the model serves as a way for the individual more easily to grasp the consequences entailed in the theory. One of my colleagues, for example, cannot follow an argument by another colleague until he translates it into a geometrical picture. The first colleague, on the other hand, has to translate the other's arguments into algebraic symbolism before he "understands" the point being made.

Another *psychological* feature of explanation that runs through this chapter is the problem of commitment to the established or accepted interpretative system. In spite of the current emphasis on creativity in research, the history of science seems to indicate that progress is made by working within the accepted pattern of explanation and methodology. Consensus among scientists about which problems are appropriate, what kinds of explanatory systems are acceptable, and what types of methods to employ in gathering the data seems to be an important element in scientific progress.* Perhaps this is because much talent and effort is simultaneously concentrated on thoroughly exploiting one narrow segment of a domain at once. Such an exhaustive mining of one claim, before moving on to another, may be the most efficient way of articulating a current system and of eventually overthrowing it. As Kuhn has pointed out, it is only when people are thoroughly committed to a system that they will devote the necessary and painstaking effort to track down the slightest anomalies within that system that still need clarification. And it is just this concern with what an outsider might consider to be a trivial deviation that eventually leads to the most convincing evidence that the system must be wrong. Scientific revolutions, if this account is correct, are brought about by internal factors rather than by invasion from without.

* See T. S. Kuhn. *The structure of scientific revolutions.* Chicago: University of Chicago Press, 1962.

Communicating
the Results

"Our language, in fact, is only approximate, and even in science it is so indefinite that if we lose sight of phenomena and cling to words, we are speedily outside of reality." (Claude Bernard, 1865.)

In trying to capture the "nature" of psychological inquiry we have treated it as being essentially the same as any other kind of scientific inquiry. The adjective "psychological" becomes important for characterizing how psychologists get their information when the subject matter or conceptual system imparts specific features to the method of research. Secondly, we have treated

7

psychological inquiry as a process, or *activity,* that extends in time and involves a continual interplay between the psychologist and his environment. We looked for the "nature" of this process by breaking down the psychologist's research activity into separate components, or *phases.* In a sense, these phases define psychological inquiry.

Psychological inquiry, in these terms, is a process of getting ideas, gathering facts with respect to these ideas, arranging and describing the facts, and interpreting or explaining these facts. Each of these aspects of inquiry is essential to its nature. But all these phases together would not make the process scientific unless the results were *communicated* and *shared* with others. Above all else, scientific inquiry is a *social* enterprise.

FROM PRIVATE TO PUBLIC WORLDS

Again and again, as we have pointed out with each of the separate phases, as a particular area of science develops from infancy to maturity, its essential features become more and more objective, formal, conventional, and abstract. In getting his ideas and sudden insights for a new way of grappling with his problem, an investigator relies on subjective, intuitive, private and essentially noncommunicable sources. He may employ highly idiosyncratic imagery, mental models, unconscious tendencies, and other intuitive devices. But when he attempts to bring his intuitions into the scientific arena, when he wishes to demonstrate their correctness, he first has to transform them into public, communicable, symbolic form. He has to put his idea into words or other public symbols. By the time the scientist has put an intuition into a communicable, *testable* form, it has lost much of its original richness and imagery. In making his idea public he has been forced to leave behind the private, noncommunicable matrix out of which it emerged. This private world serves as his source of ideas; but he depends on the socially shared standards of the scientific community to help him decide if his idea has value. The scientist knows that his idea may be a candidate for the special domain of scientific knowledge only when he can formulate it completely within the approved, public language of the scientific community.

This same transition from private to public world can be shown for each of the other phases of inquiry. As the scientist moves from the natural-history stage of his inquiry into the later and more clearly scientific stages, his observational basis must shift from a reliance on casual and private experience to a dependence on public and socially shared observation. The criterion of reproducibility of scientific observation is nothing but the requirement that scientific data must be restricted to those facts upon which universal agreement or consensus can be achieved. This criterion of objectivity, in the final analysis, is a social one; an "objective fact" is simply one that can be shared by different individuals. The procedures for reducing, describing, and testing data also reflect the development from subjective to objective methods. Piaget and Skinner, for example, ask us to rely on their private judgment as they place before us what they consider to be typical cases of the results they obtain. Unfortunately, such descriptions of the data, depending as they do on special characteristics of the investigator, do not allow for a unique characterization of the outcome. A different investigator, playing with the same total set of data, might select different cases or features as representative. As an inquiry moves towards maturity, we see forms of analysis and data-reduction that not only are much more explicit and standardized but also tend to guarantee a unique outcome for each set of data. The object, as with the development in all of the phases, is to approximate an ideal where the outcome and the description are completely independent of the peculiar characteristics of the individual investigator. In the interpretation phase of inquiry, the maturational sequence makes its way from personal analogies and models through explicit, shared models and ultimately to completely abstract, symbolic summaries of a domain of experience.

Jean Piaget, L. S. Vigotsky, A. R. Luria and other developmental psychologists have explicitly or implicitly suggested that the development of thinking in children follows a developmental pattern much like the development of communication within science. At first a child approaches reality through the immediate, perceptually dominant aspects of the situation. As he grows from infancy to the walking stage, he gradually develops some independence from immediate perceptual dominance; he learns, for example, that when an object is hidden behind a pillow it persists rather than disappears. He learns to recognize familiar faces and respond accordingly. With further development, he gains a mastery over conceptual classifications and is able, on an intuitive level, to symbolize and internalize some aspects of his environment. He is able to employ words, for example, to explain why things are so, but he is not interested in verifying or demonstrating his explanations. Only in adolescence does the child begin to employ formal modes of thinking and become concerned with explaining and accounting for circumstances instead of just dealing with events as they force themselves on his immediate attention. If the picture on the television tube temporarily goes out, the ten-year-old child might be capable of trying out various manipulations of dials and antenna, in an attempt to regain the picture. If the picture does come back, the problem-solving process ends. He has achieved his goal, and does not wonder beyond this. At an older age, at a more mature level of development, the child will be concerned not only with getting back the picture but also with reasons why the picture disappeared and why it returned.

Piaget and the Russian psychologists independently agree that this important development of thought is a direct result of the child's communicating with adults and peers. In gradually achieving mastery of public, as opposed to private, forms of representing the world, the child simultaneously can internalize a system by which he can check his private thoughts against those of his culture. By recasting his ideas into language, and, in a sense, carrying out a conversation with himself, the child gradually achieves a stage of development in which he can view the world from a point other than his own private one. The late Russian psychologist Vigotsky actually did experiments which demonstrated that, at certain stages, when a child is put in a difficult situation he will carry on a dialogue with himself as if he were trying to reconstruct his parent to find out what help or advice would come from that source.

The movement from private to public modes of symbolizing and representing one's ideas, then, seems to be an important step in the development of an individual's thinking as well as in the development of a science. Both individual and scientific thinking depend heavily on arriving at results and actions that can be shared with other members of the community. The gradual socialization of the child, during which he slowly internalizes and masters the public language of his culture, can be seen as an indoctrination process that enables him to anticipate and understand how others would view certain behaviors and ideas. It allows the child to become aware of other viewpoints, to see things from the eyes of others, and thereby to be able to adjust and interact with others as a member of society. Scientific communication serves a similar function. By mastering the specialized framework and vocabulary of science, the scientist can recast his ideas and thoughts into this public mode, not only as a way of communicating them to others, but also as a way of looking upon his ideas from another viewpoint—one that is shared by the specialized subculture to which he as a scientist belongs.

THE VALUE OF COMMUNICATING

This attempt—to make his reports intelligible to a general public, or at least to the psychological profession as a whole, while at the same time trying to approximate the scientific ideals of precise and objective terminology—creates a variety of problems. There is the communication gap between the psychologist and the general public; there is the publication explosion resulting from the pressures to publish and the geometrically increasing rate of growth of the psychological profession; there is the possible hampering effect of the formalities of scientific communication on scientific creativity; and there is the other side of the coin, the possible values to the scientist himself of communicating his results to others.

Because the negative side of the problem has received much attention, we shall deal here only with some of the positive values of the communication problem—especially with the effects of the strict limitations imposed on the scientist when he wishes to communicate his results.

The recasting of his ideas into the impersonal and conventional mold dictated by publication policy is an important aspect of a psychologist's thinking.

As we pointed out when we drew the analogy between the development of scientific thinking and the development of children's thinking, the evidence seems to indicate that thought reaches its highest form of precision and objectivity when it is forced into highly formalized symbols and structures. Quite frequently the investigator only fully realizes the implications of his work when he finally sits down at the typewriter and attempts to rearrange his thoughts into the standardized and logical format required by the journal article.

In his article on the development of his conception of motivation, Hebb makes the following remark, "While writing this paper I found myself having to make a change in my own theoretical position." * The famous biologist, J. Z. Young begins a book of lectures with these words: †

The scientist does not usually think of the writing of books or preparing of lectures as research. Writing seems to him to be a rather tiresome labor that he must do after the fun of laboratory research and discovery is over. I therefore sat down to use the time available more in hope of making a summary than a discovery. But when I began to do this I came to realize the extent to which having to describe the results of one's thoughts to others is a part of the process of discovery itself. We are social creatures, depending far more than we realize on communication with each other. We can understand better both the workings of the brain and the nature of scientific inquiry itself if we realize how deeply our whole life is influenced by this necessity of communication. Paying attention to this fact has made me think in a way that is new and helpful to me, and I hope may be so for others also.

One result of preparing one's thoughts for publication is that the very impersonal terminology and format the writer must employ helps him to achieve what Piaget calls "decentering"—a move away from seeing the inquiry and its results from one's own, personal viewpoint towards a neutral, dispassionate viewpoint. Secondly, the necessity of translating one's thinking into more conventional terminology often separates the connotations of one's own mental imagery from those actually implied by the relations among the data. Such translation helps an investigator to free his ideas from the particularization of the concrete imagery and phrasing he happened to employ in conceptualizing his research to himself.

Even the severe limitation of allowable space in professional journals provides a positive incentive to clear thinking. By being forced to reduce his complex study to its bare bones, a psychologist has to struggle within himself —and the term "struggle" in this context is not chosen lightly—to decide which of the many many facets are really the important ones and which can be ignored. Contrary to the repeated complaints that this enforced space limitation seriously dampens creativity, the reverse might actually be true.

* D. P. Hebb. Drives and C. N. S. (conceptual nervous system). *Psychol. Rev.*, 1955, 62, 243–254.
† J. Z. Young. *Doubt and certainty in science.* New York: Oxford University Press, 1960, p. 1.

There is no disputing the fact that a selection must be made: however great our activity, facts outstrip us, and we can never overtake them; while the scientist is discovering one fact, millions and millions are produced in every cubic inch of his body. Trying to make science contain nature is like trying to make the part contain the whole.

Later in the same volume, Poincaré, whom I have just quoted, says, "Discovery is discernment, selection." *

In addition to the impetus to rearrangement of thinking that preparing journal articles can have, similiar effects have been reported as a result of discussing ideas with students or colleagues. Having to answer a question posed by a student can often be the stimulus for suddenly realizing that you have been overlooking an important relationship in your data. A colleague reported that after having given the same lecture for two years, one in which he employed some of his own data to illustrate a point he was making, a question by a student made him pause and suddenly realize that, in fact, his data actually supported an alternative interpretation rather than the one he had been making for the previous two years.

A vivid illustration of how the necessity of having to put oneself in another's shoes in order to get across a point can lead to a scientific discovery is illustrated in the case of the floppy-eared rabbits.† This is a true and contemporary history of how two medical researchers, at approximately the same time, independently came across the same striking phenomenon—the sudden wilting of a rabbit's ears after injection by the enzyme papain. Both men immediately attempted to find an explanation for this phenomenon. Both failed.

Some time after this original incident, one of the researchers returned to the phenomenon of the floppy-ears and solved the mystery. Two socioligists were fortunate enough to hear about the case and to obtain detailed interviews with both of the men who were independently involved. The report illustrates several different aspects of how inquiry is actually done and how discoveries are made. But for our purposes, we are interested in only one feature, one which is relevant to the role of having to communicate one's thinking and findings to others.

One of the researchers, Dr. Lewis Thomas, as an incidental feature of some research he was conducting, happened to inject the enzyme papain into a rabbit and noticed the spectacular flopping of the ears that resulted. He immediately tried to track down the explanation. He did the expected. He sliced and stained the rabbit's ears. He could find nothing unusual in the connective tissue where one would expect to find changes. He also looked at the cartilage, but could see nothing obvious. As he himself tells it, he had

* H. Poincaré. *Science and method.* New York: Dover, undated reprint of 1914 translation.

† B. Barber, and Renee C. Fox. The case of the floppy-eared rabbits: an instance of serendipity gained and serendipity lost. *Amer. J. Sociology,* 1958, 64, 128–136.

always looked on cartilage as relatively inactive and uninteresting. He would certainly have not expected to find the answer in the cartilage. Dr. Aaron Kellner, the other researcher who independently came across this same phenomenon, also overlooked the cartilage because of the same expectations about its inertness.

Approximately seven years later, however, Dr. Thomas was teaching second-year medical students, showing the kind of research scientists perform in the laboratory. As an example of how scientists go after a problem, Thomas thought of demonstrating the floppy-eared phenomenon. Because it was spectacular he felt it would entertain and capture the students' interest. The students, as expected, took a keen interest in the demonstration. As Thomas put it:

> Well, this time I did what I didn't do before. I simultaneously cut sections of the ears of rabbits after I'd given them papain *and* sections of normal ears. This is the part of the story I'm most ashamed of. It still makes me writhe to think of it. There was no damage to the tissue in the sense of a lesion. But what had taken place was a quantitative change in the matrix of the cartilage. The only way you could make sense of this change was simultaneously to compare sections taken from the ears of rabbits which had been injected with papain with comparable sections from the ears of rabbits of the same age and size which had not received papain.

Note what has happened. In the normal course of his research, Thomas, as any experienced and effective researcher does, takes many short-cuts and skips steps that are formally necessary, but which often waste time. He uses his backlog of previous experience and experimental know-how to attend to what is most likely and to treat casually aspects that are least likely to be important. In this particular case, the strong and generally justified assumption that cartilage was inactive led him to carry out that portion of his search with less care than he would urge on others. Only when he had to demonstrate how one should look for changes in cartilage by the textbook procedure of comparing slices of tissue from treated and untreated animals did he discover the flaw in his prior search for an answer. Here we see a case where the necessity to alter his thinking, or rearrange his approach, to fit into an approved mode uncovered a hidden assumption and enabled a researcher to make an important discovery.

In a similar fashion, as we have urged in this chapter, the necessity to reorder one's thinking to conform with standard and publicly dictated forms may frequently uncover flaws or hidden assumptions in the psychologist's interpretations and may serve to give him new insights into what he has been dealing with.

CONCLUSION

The process of inquiry, then, consists of a series of activities that enable the scientist to work his way from vague, subjective hunches to explicit, objective statements about phenomena. Although each of the activities is essential to the success of the total enterprise, it is the activity of communicating and sharing the fruits of inquiry with others that controls and gives scientific inquiry its special flavor. It is because of the need and desire to convey his findings to his colleagues that the scientist becomes interested in objectivity, proof, and explicit formulation. And it is this struggle for the kind of formulation that will be both exact and yet consonant with his private world that continually goads the scientist to struggle for better ways to summarize and codify what we know today and what we will know tomorrow.

Selected Readings

General

Bachrach, A. J. *Psychological research: an introduction.* New York: Random House, 1962 (Paperback).

Bernard, C. *An introduction to the study of experimental medicine.* New York: Dover, 1957 (Paperback).

Beveridge, W. I. B. *The art of scientific investigation.* (Revised ed.). New York: Random House, 1957 (Paperback).

Brown, C. W., and E. E. Ghiselli. *Scientific method in psychology.* New York: McGraw-Hill, 1955.

Scott, W. A., and M. Wertheimer. *Introduction to psychological research.* New York: Wiley, 1962.

Wilson, E. B. *An introduction to scientific research.* New York: McGraw-Hill, 1952.

Chapters 1 and 2

Boring, E. G. *A history of experimental psychology* (Second ed.). New York: Appleton-Century-Crofts, 1950.

Garrett, H. E. *Great experiments in psychology* (Third ed.). New York: Appleton-Century-Crofts, 1951.

Kemeny, J. G. *A philosopher looks at science.* Princeton: Van Nostrand, 1959.

Chapter 3

Cohen, I. B. *Science, servant of man.* Boston: Little, Brown, 1950.

Conant, J. B. (ed.). *Harvard case histories in experimental science.* Cambridge: Harvard University Press, 1957.

Dubos, R. *Louis Pasteur: free lance of science.* Boston: Little, Brown, 1950.

Gillispie, C. C. *The edge of objectivity*. Princeton: Princeton University Press, 1960.

Hadamard, J. *The psychology of invention in the mathematical field*. Princeton: Princeton University Press, 1945 (Dover paperback reprint).

Koestler, A. *The watershed: a biography of Johannes Kepler*. New York: Anchor, 1960 (Paperback).

Taton, R. *Reason and chance in scientific discovery*. New York: Science Editions, 1962 (Paperback).

Chapter 4

Andrews, T. G. (ed.). *Methods of psychology*. New York: Wiley, 1948.

Vogt, E. Z., and R. Hyman. *Waterwitching U.S.A.* Chicago: University of Chicago Press, 1959.

Woodworth, R. S., and H. Schlosberg. *Experimental psychology* (Revised ed.). New York: Holt, Rinehart and Winston, 1954.

Chapter 5

Bross, I. D. J. *Design for decision*. New York: Macmillan, 1953.

Huff, D. *How to lie with statistics*. New York: Norton, 1954.

Moroney, M. J. *Facts from figures*. (Second ed.). London: Penguin, 1953 (Paperback).

Chapter 6

Brunswick, E. Ontogenetic and other developmental parallels to the history of science. In H. M. Evans (ed.). *Men and moments in the history of science*. Seattle: University of Washington Press, 1959, pp. 3–21.

Hanson, N. R. *Patterns of discovery*. Cambridge: Cambridge University Press, 1961.

Kuhn, T. S. *The structure of scientific revolutions*. Chicago: University of Chicago Press, 1962.

Marx, M. H. (ed.). *Theories in contemporary psychology*. New York: Macmillan, 1963.

Nagel, E. *The structure of science*. New York: Harcourt, Brace & World, 1961.

Chapter 7

Mandler, G., and W. Kessen. *The language of psychology*. New York: Wiley, 1959.

Young, J. Z. *Doubt and certainty in science*. New York: Oxford University Press, 1960 (Paperback).

Index